She Dances to Different Drums

Research into disabled women's sexuality

Kath Gillespie-Sells, Mildrette Hill, Bree Robbins
SHE uk (Sexual Health and Equality) of Disabled Women

King's **Fund**

Published by
King's Fund Publishing
11–13 Cavendish Square
London W1M 0AN

© King's Fund 1998

First published 1998

ISBN 1 85717 158 6

A CIP catalogue record for this book is available from the British Library

Distributed by Grantham Book Services Limited
Isaac Newton Way
Alma Park Industrial Estate
GRANTHAM
Lincolnshire
NG31 9SD

Tel: 01476 541 080
Fax: 01476 541 061

Printed and bound in Great Britain

Cover image: Lizi Stuart

Contents

This book is dedicated to Millee Hill,
who tragically died before its publication.
She will always be missed.

Acknowledgements

SHE uk would like to thank the King's Fund for having made this research possible. They took a leap of faith in funding this non-traditional piece of research – the first of its kind – thereby supporting the creativity of the disabled women who contributed to this project. In taking this step, the King's Fund have acknowledged the isolation which disabled women experience in expressing their sexuality and given them a platform to voice their fears, traumas, expectations, delights and hopes. This research has set in motion a growing network which disabled women can use to redefine their sexuality.

Thanks also to Mildrette Hill for her artistic work which provided SHE uk with the drawings in this report; to Char March for giving us her poems, which have been included; and to Dilis Clare for reading all our drafts and then editing this report.

Finally, we would like to thank Deborah Hart from Microsyster for all her advice and help with the software and for teaching us how to input the data and analyse the questionnaires.

Disclaimer

About the authors

Mildrette Hill is co-founder of the Black Disabled People's Association, established in 1990 and founder member of the Black Spectrum 1995, an organisation and consultancy of black disabled people. She is also a member of a number of other disability and race and disability organisations. She has a combined honours degree from York University, Toronto, Canada, and a master's degree from the New York Institute of Technology. She is a student barrister and research writer with a number of publications on politico-economic, legislation and law, and race and disability issues.

Acknowledgements

I would like to thank Margaret Brown, Mary-Beth Aitken, Maria Oshodi and Almundena Hague for their invaluable support and advice. I would also like to express my sincere thanks to all those black disabled women who gave so generously of their time and so unselfishly of their secrets in support of this research.

Kath Gillespie-Sells was the founding member of REGARD, the campaigning organisation of disabled lesbians and gay men established in 1989 to address the heterosexism that exists within the disability movement/community. Kath is a specialist adviser in the area of welfare rights for disabled people and is a freelance training consultant. She is a researcher and author. Recent publications include chapters in H. Curtis (ed.), *Sexual Health Promotion in General Practice* (Oxford: Radcliffe Medical Press, 1995), and in Trevillion & Beresford (eds.), *Meeting The Challenge: social work education and the community care revolution* (London: National Institute for Social Work, 1996). Recent endeavours include co-authorship of *Untold Desires: Politics of disability and sexuality* (Cassells, 1997). Kath's background is in health and education. She is a counsellor with PACE, the Project Advice Counselling and Education for lesbians and gay men. Kath also counsels in a North London health clinic.

Acknowledgements

I would like to thank all the lesbians and bisexual women who took part in this research. A special thanks to the women who were prepared to be interviewed and share painful memories, difficult times and liberating experiences in their powerful testimonies. Special thanks to Dilis for her support throughout the project and for her intensive input toward the end of the project to achieve the desired edited version of the report. Thanks also to Jenny for her support and determination and financial wizardry in maintaining the SHE accounts. Special thanks also to James for his many successful rescues and solutions when 'computer seemed to be winning over woman' ...

Bree Robbins has been involved with a number of organisations of disabled people, including the British Council of Organisations of Disabled People, Ealing Access Group, Union of the Physically Impaired Against Segregation, and Disabled People Against Apartheid. She is a freelance training consultant.

She has been an adviser to two London boroughs and has run training courses in community care, stress management, disabled women and service delivery. She has also been responsible for training for trainers in DET and access training. She is currently training in personal development. She was commissioned to write a section on disabled people's sexuality for the Open University's course *The Disability Society* (K665), published in 1993.

She has a BA Hons in developmental psychology from Sussex University. She has completed a course on hypnotherapy from the British Council of Hypnotist Examiners and a self-hypnosis diploma course from the Merjon School of Therapeutic Hypnosis. She has also completed a course with Denise Linn on past life regressions. Bree counsels in hypnotherapy and teaches self-hypnosis.

Acknowledgements

I would like to thank all the disabled women who agreed to meet and talk about their most intimate moments. Some of the memories were painful, some happy, but all have inspired us to continue working together to make changes that would empower our lives. I would also like to thank all of the thousands of disabled women that we have not met, for whom this report was written. Thanks also to Deborah for all the hours we spent setting up the database, and for helping me to cope when the pivot tables and charts seemed to take forever to create.

Glossary

Black disabled woman: any woman of African, Caribbean or Asian origin who has obvious or hidden impairments, who experiences mental health difficulties or who has AIDS or is HIV-positive.

Bisexual woman: a woman whose sexual choices are with both men and women.

Class: the rank or social order of persons.

Disability: the reversible loss or limitation of opportunity to take part in the normal life of the community on an equal basis owing to institutional, environmental or attitudinal barriers.

Disability movement: the collective of disabled individuals, disability organisations, groups and representatives actively engaged in campaigning for the attainment of civil rights for disabled people and highlighting issues of concern to them.

Disabled woman: any woman who has obvious or hidden impairments, who experiences mental health difficulties, or who has AIDS or is HIV-positive.

Disablism: the institutional discrimination and exclusion that disabled people experience because of their impairments.

Heterosexism: an institutionalised belief in the inherent superiority of the heterosexual pattern of loving.

Heterosexual woman: a woman whose sexual choice is to be with men. This encompasses the privileges of the dominant sexual culture.

Homophobia: the irrational fear of feelings of love for members of one's own sex and therefore the hatred of those feelings in others.

Impairment: a loss of or limitation in an individual's physical, mental or sensory function.

Lesbian: a woman whose lifestyle, emotional and sexual choice is to be with women.

Racism: an institutionalised and irrational belief in the inherent superiority of one race over others.

Sexism: an institutionalised belief in the inherent superiority of one sex over another.

Special schools: schools which cater wholly for pupils with so-called 'special educational needs', e. g. disabled pupils.

Obituary

In loving memory of our friend Millee Hill,
who died on Monday 24 November 1997, at her home in London,
and was buried in her beloved Bermuda on 4 December 1997.

Her tenacious campaigning for the rights of disabled people
and tireless advocacy for Black disabled people in particular,
along with her contribution to the debate on disability art,
will be a tremendous loss to all of us.

Her intelligence, wit, indomitable spirit and deep caring
was a true inspiration that we will sadly miss.

Maria Oshodi

Introduction

The SHE uk (Sexual Health and Equality) project is the first major piece of research on disabled women's sexuality undertaken in the UK by *disabled women researchers*. During a workshop on sexuality at the 1992 GLAD (Greater London Association of Disabled People) disabled women's conference, so many issues were raised that the facilitators – Gillespie-Sells and Robbins – decided to initiate this ground-breaking piece of work. Hill, the third researcher, who was a participant at that workshop, was approached to gather the views and responses of black disabled women. Funding to carry out the study was secured from the King's Fund.

The idea of research into disabled women's sexuality had been around for quite some time having been publicly aired as far back as 1986 at the closing conference of the GLC (the Greater London Council, abolished in 1986). Over the years, disabled women in their support groups and fora have discussed the social isolation that they have experienced. They have voiced the opinion that their sexuality is often threatened or dismissed, while some have even felt that their sexuality was out of their own individual control.

While acknowledging some positive developments in the liberation of disabled people, disabled women were expressing feelings of dissatisfaction and frustration that the issue of sexuality was not on the agenda of many disability organisations; nor was it being accorded the attention from leading spokespersons on disability issues that they felt it deserved. Increasingly, disabled women were expressing the wish that something be done to address the yawning gaps in literature, support networks and other resources dealing with disability and sexuality. In taking up the challenge, the SHE researchers have attempted to address some of those concerns.

The fact that there is a great deal of negativity, prejudice and misunderstanding about disabled women's sexuality is irrefutable; also irrefutable is the fact that these misconceptions can have a very negative impact upon the lives of disabled women. The many barriers to and restrictions on the positive exploration and expression of their sexual identity only serve to worsen what is for many of them an existence already blighted by other difficulties. The dearth of information on disabled women's sexuality only aggravates the situation. The encouragement of disabled women to explore and express their sexuality and the documentation of their shared experiences must surely go some way to improving the situation.

Confronting the difficulties

In attempting to explore and highlight the issues surrounding disabled women's sexuality, the researchers were aware that they would be violating one of the last great taboos. Disability and sexuality remains a controversial subject capable of provoking extreme reaction, misunderstanding and prejudice. Thus, although many disabled women had over the years expressed the need for research into disability and sexuality, the researchers' expectations were that there would be some difficulties, resistance and even opposition – and so there was!

However, no one could have anticipated just how extremely difficult it would actually prove to see the project through to fruition. Ironically, the researchers encountered many difficulties from the most unexpected quarter, namely the SHE uk advisory group.

The advisory group

During the research an advisory group was appointed to help to support the researchers and guide the project. Each researcher selected two women from her target group. Thus, there were two disabled lesbians, two disabled heterosexual women and two black disabled women, in addition to the three researchers. The group was to meet quarterly.

Unfortunately, shortly after the work had begun, much of the support that the researchers had hoped would come from the advisers began to wither away. Only two of the appointees remained committed to the project through to the end. The others failed to support the project, usually citing other issues going on in the disability movement to which they said they would prefer to direct their energies. Thus the researchers were obliged to call upon support from other experienced individuals as and when it was required.

Opposition

Given the sensitive nature of the research it was expected that some disabled women would decline to participate. However, some of the various reasons given for non-participation had not been expected and took even the researchers quite by surprise. For example, one disabled woman who refused to take part cited her belief that disabled women were not able to form sexual relationships: the reason given was her conviction that men were not attracted to disabled women because they neglected their personal hygiene.

Another disabled woman declined to participate because she said that such research should be carried out by medical experts. Still another refused, or more precisely was not allowed to participate because she said her husband did not approve of that type of thing. Other disabled women declined on the grounds that there were far more important issues going on in the disability movement to which the researchers should be directing their energies. Yet more said that the research should have been undertaken by other, 'more qualified' researchers.

There was also some lack of co-operation from a number of representatives of disability organisations. Indulging in a spot of self-policing, a few stubbornly refused to send out the questionnaires, thereby effectively denying their disabled women members the opportunity to determine for themselves whether or not they wished to contribute to the research. One such representative, when challenged, stated that she knew all of the disabled women in her organisation and was certain that absolutely none of them was interested in sex, sexuality or sexual matters.

Happily, there was, on the other hand, a great deal of enthusiasm and support from many disabled women who felt that the SHE research was a worthwhile, necessary and long-overdue endeavour. They expressed their satisfaction that at last someone was prepared to address these difficult issues and attempt to document disabled women's views on their sexuality and collateral issues.

The sample

The research was designed *specifically* to focus in on three target groups. It aimed to gauge the opinions and experiences of lesbian, heterosexual, and black disabled women above school-leaving age, across the different impairments and across the country. The findings were to be gathered from questionnaires, interviews and small group seminars.

It was decided to confine the initial study to England. This was a pragmatic decision as it was thought that the cultural differences in Scotland, Wales and Ireland would make this initial research too large to handle. However, some requests and responses came from other areas of the UK. These have been included in the statistical data and some form part of the information gathered from the interviews.

The women invited to complete the questionnaires were not approached directly by the researchers. However, some women contacted SHE directly to request questionnaires and to take part in the project. The researchers were particularly concerned to reach out to and make contact with disabled women who did not have a 'high profile' or established presence within the disability movement.

Thus, different means had to be employed in an effort to reach some of the more isolated disabled women who were perhaps not already associated with an established organisation. In order to achieve this, approximately 18 months into the project, the researchers funded a seminar to which selected women from the three target groups were invited. The aim was to gather further information from the participants and to test their reaction to the research findings (see Appendix 1).

The questionnaire

The questionnaire was devised by the researchers who took advice from a variety of sources, including other disabled women and disabled professionals and researchers. One disabled researcher advised them not to use questionnaires as he was of the opinion that they were usually thrown in the bin. However, after some consideration, the researchers persisted because they felt that it was one way and possibly the only way to involve certain disabled women. A pilot study with twelve women was carried out in order to test the questionnaires.

After minor amendments, 1,000 questionnaires were printed. In order to ensure confidentiality and anonymity, the questionnaires (see Appendix 2) were sent to disability and other organisations around the country with an explanatory letter and the request that they be forwarded to their disabled women members. In addition to the questionnaire, the pack included a letter of introduction, guidance notes and a stamped addressed envelope. Much depended on the goodwill of the organisations to forward the packs so several months later a follow-up letter was sent to the organisations. Eighteen per cent of the questionnaires were returned completed.

On average, 33 per cent of research questionnaires were returned. As this was the first major work of this type there was no norm and it was therefore difficult to interpret or assess the SHE response rate. Further research needs to be carried out before a more definitive commentary on the response can be made.

The interviews

Some of the women who agreed to the interviews were self-selecting in that they indicated on their completed questionnaire that they wished to be interviewed. Others were approached directly by the researchers and invited to undergo interview.

Confidentiality was deemed to be of the utmost importance in carrying out the research. It was anticipated that the women who volunteered to be interviewed would need to feel safe and free to express their feelings and some would require at least one follow-up, if not more. Thus tact, caution and a 'softly softly' approach were considered to be important.

The researchers

The three researchers were themselves disabled women who through self-definition and personal experience were able to identify themselves with the three target groups. Therefore, for the most part, disabled lesbians and bisexual women were in contact with and interviewed by SHE's lesbian researcher, while the black disabled women participants were interviewed by SHE's black researcher, and the heterosexual women by SHE's heterosexual researcher.

However, given the multifarious aspects of an individual's character, naturally a number of women fell into more than one or even into all three of the categories. For example, there were a number of women who described themselves as disabled, black and lesbian or disabled, black and heterosexual or bisexual, and so on. These women were offered a choice of which researcher they preferred to be interviewed by.

Hypotheses

The researchers drew up a set of hypotheses based on the comments and opinions of disabled women, anecdotal evidence and observations of the disabled communities.

The research sought to test the hypotheses listed below.

1. That there is inadequate sex education and information available to disabled girls and women, particularly those who were born disabled.

2. That those disabled women who acquired a disability later in life are more likely to be in a sexual relationship or have had sexual partners.

3. That the race and religion of disabled women will influence their sexual choices and freedom to explore them.

4. That a disabled woman's ability to express her sexuality is greatly influenced by her exposure, or lack thereof, to information about sexual choices.

5. That disabled women are more likely than non-disabled women to experience sexual abuse.

6. That disabled women lack positive role models to improve self-esteem.

7. That disabled women do not practise safer sex.

8. That disabled women are reluctant to talk to each other about sex but will talk to other people about it.

Methodology

What little disability and sexuality research had been previously undertaken had been carried out largely by non-disabled professionals. As a result, there were very few sources to which the researchers could turn for specific guidance, assistance or advice. They were therefore obliged to look overseas where some guidance came in the form of a research document on women with learning difficulties and sexuality carried out by a group of disabled women called DAWN Canada.

Thus, quite early into the project the researchers became aware that the research would not easily lend itself to the sociological approach usually adopted. Instead they allowed the research to be guided by what disabled women themselves considered important.

The process

There are to be at least two phases to the research with each phase divided into several parts. To date only the first phase has been funded.

Phase 1 was to run over two years and consisted of:

- The appointment of advisers to the researchers to support and critically assess the research.
- Questionnaires devised and a pilot study conducted in order to test them.
- The questionnaire and in-depth interview stage for disabled women in the UK.
- The setting-up of a database.
- The hosting of a fully funded seminar for invited women from the target groups.
- The compilation of a research document on the Phase 1 findings.

Future plans include:

- The establishment of support networks and other resources.
- Additional research further afield.
- Phase 2 seminars for invited individuals and target groups.
- The compilation and publication of additional research findings.
- The consolidation of SHE uk as a permanent source of support and information.
- The production of a video on disabled women's sexuality.

This publication

The following chapters represent the findings of research into issues regarding the sexuality of black, lesbian and heterosexual disabled women. All the evidence and testimony was gathered from disabled women from a range of ages and a variety of backgrounds. Although disabled women are not always a distinct and monolithic group, there are some issues which are common to all of them. This is because disability and sexuality cut right across all the different class, cultural, racial, religious and age categories of the female population. Thus, there are some issues such as access to sex education, role models and attitudinal barriers which naturally feature in all three chapters, just as there are some issues which contrast sharply from chapter to chapter.

Also, the three themes of *image and invisibility* , *abuse* and *mothering* seemed to have such important ramifications for disabled women's sexuality that they warranted additional comment beyond that given by the women in the main text.

Chapter 1

The daughters of warrior women

Black disabled women and sexuality

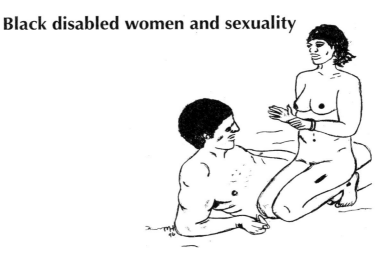

This chapter focuses on black disabled women. This is defined as women of African, Caribbean or Asian origin who have visible or hidden impairments, or who experience mental health difficulties. The primary findings of this part of the SHE research were gathered from the 10 per cent of black disabled women who returned their completed questionnaires, from in-depth one-to-one interviews and from some follow-up discussions with ten black disabled women. Additional information was gathered from written submissions, the SHE seminar, and informal discussions with 18 disabled women.

To some extent, therefore, the study is a representation of those women's own experiences from their unique and specific positions, though all the women remain anonymous and pseudonyms are used throughout. However, the research is not merely a collection of personal stories and thus cannot be said to be strictly biographical. Sexual health cannot be separated from its wider social, political, educational and cultural contexts.

The study seeks to provide a broader overview of the things which affect black disabled women's sexuality. In addition to their personal stories of their interior lives, it examines some of the external factors which shape the experiences of black disabled women and have an impact upon their sexuality and sexual expression.

Setting the context

Frequently, the reality of black disabled women's lives contrasts sharply with other people's perceptions of them. Their own hopes and aspirations repeatedly clash with the expectations which others have set. As one of the women put it,

> *Just because I am disabled, people think they have the right to tell me how to live my life, but often what they want for me is not what I want for myself at all. Because of this, I am often fighting against other people's views of me. As a black disabled woman, it seems that every time I want something, I have to fight for it. All of my energy is spent in fighting for things and it doesn't half tick me off at times.*

As all the women quoted in this chapter identified as black and disabled, there were naturally many common themes which were present in their experiences. However, there was no golden thread which ran throughout and bound them all together into a homogeneous whole. Each woman was individual and different and spoke on behalf of only herself. The study therefore does not purport to represent a 'universal' view of black disabled women's sexuality. It simply looks at some of their more common experiences and aims to show how many misconceptions are often perpetuated and sustained by popular belief.

All of the women who were interviewed agreed that sexuality encompassed many different aspects of life, of which sex was only a part. Sexuality is a combination of the physical and spiritual parts of one's being. Sexual health is when they come together in ways which enrich and enhance one's personality, self-esteem and self-confidence. As one of the women said,

> *The sexual part of me is only a small part of what constitutes my sexuality, therefore when discussing sexuality you have to consider so many other things as well.*

Primary focus

Black disabled women have many different parts to their identities. Therefore, within the constraints of this study, it is impossible to deal in great depth with all the influences which shape and inform their sexuality. Of necessity, I have focused primarily on only a few of the main areas which the women themselves identified. Thus, some important issues such as class, employment and age have not been dealt with in any depth.

Highlighted and examined is the pressure exerted on black disabled women by their family, their formative education, their religion and culture and the social convention of heterosexual relationships. The important effects on the women's sexuality of their impairment and disability are also discussed. In addition, the positive experience of support from friends and school mates and association with other black disabled women is explored.

Myths and stereotypes

Myths and stereotypes distort and misrepresent the reality of black disabled women's sexuality, oversimplifying their real lives. Stereotypes which typically define black disabled women are that they are asexual, unlovable and unfit for any man to marry. In contrast, stereotypical images of black able-bodied women are that they are sexy, exotic, mysterious and desirable. These stereotypes inform people's attitudes and responses towards them. Black disabled women are frequently caught between these two diametrically opposed misrepresentations: they are often unsure against which one they are being measured and which image it is they are not living up to. Yet these attitudes can influence the nature and quality of the individual woman's sexual experiences. More than 70 per cent of the women interviewed acknowledged the fact that external factors have an influence on an individual's sexuality. For example, Ujima is a single woman in her early forties who became disabled at the age of twelve. She says,

> As black disabled women we are to some extent what society makes us or what society allows us to be, whether we like it or not. Look at me: I would like to have got married and had children but there were so many forces working against me that it never happened, and it wasn't from want of trying, let me tell you. It really makes me angry when I think that there is so much going on out there that we have no control over … yet it is able to control us and what we do in our lives.
>
> I mean, even when it comes to disabled women having a baby, there are people out there who think that they have the right to tell you that you shouldn't simply because you're disabled. Many years ago I had an abortion that I didn't really want because everyone I told, even though it was only a few people, all said that it would be wrong for me to go ahead with it. At the time I remember my doctor telling me that I should consider being sterilised so that I wouldn't make the mistake of having another unwanted pregnancy, but the fact is that I did want it and have been wanting to have another baby ever since. When my non-disabled friend went for an abortion, her doctor didn't suggest to her that she should get sterilised.

Deconstructing the myths

Through this study, the women deconstruct some of the more common stereotypes which are attached to black disabled women; they explore the results and consequences for their sexual health of other people's misunderstandings and misconceptions. However, the women do not dwell solely on the negative outcomes. They show how it is possible to go on to create or reclaim one's own sense of self and to establish a healthy, satisfying sexual personality. As Iman said,

> There is a lot of negativity out there but that does not mean that we all go around with a cloud hanging over us all the time. We may have to fight and fight hard for it but some of us can come through with a positive sense of who we are.

From where they are

At any given time black disabled women may be experiencing several types of marginalisation or exclusion. This means that they have different experiences from those of women in groups into which they may also fall. This compounded marginalisation can have serious implications for their sexual health. It can affect the way they see themselves, the way they feel about themselves, their self-esteem and their self-confidence.

The holistic woman

Thus, black disabled women are often wrestling with more than one form of oppression. Systematic oppression includes racism, disablism, sexism and heterosexism, in combination with poverty and linguistic and cultural barriers. Raven explained it in these terms:

> *The uniqueness of black disabled women's experience means that it is different from that of white disabled women because of our race. Likewise, it is different from that of non-disabled black women because of our impairment and disability.*

Each factor alone may be enough to blight the lives of black disabled women and detract from their sexual and spiritual well-being. With a combination of factors, the hardship can be even greater. It is often difficult for others to understand why, when black disabled women are dealing with so many issues, their priorities may not be the same as other women's. Concern for sexuality and sexual health can so easily slip down the agenda when pressing issues such as employment, suitable housing, further education and adequate service provision are on the same agenda.

Athena is a grandmother who became disabled later in life and as a result is, as she put it, learning to become a black disabled activist. Having seen it from both sides, she often makes comparisons between life as a black woman and life as a black disabled woman. She feels that becoming disabled has added a new dimension to her life. She says,

> *I never used to think about these things before but I now see that the issues for black disabled women can be and often are different from other women's issues and other women don't always understand that – not even other disabled women or other black women. There are so many things that affect us as black disabled people that don't affect other people from the black and the disabled communities because they are not both black and disabled – which we are.*

For example, using your taxicard and trying to get a taxi to come on time – or at all. Most black able-bodied women won't understand that. Or trying to sort out a benefit and being asked where you come from and how long you have been living here because you have a black face and a West Indian accent and they automatically think you are trying to get something which doesn't belong to you. Most white disabled women won't know what that is like. When we have so much to worry about it's no wonder that sometimes we're just too tired to worry about sex as well – you only have so much energy. In fact, I think you should be able to go down to something like a hospital and buy sex when you need it and get rid of all that in-between stuff. It would sure cut out a lot of the problems.

Raven also describes herself as learning to become a black disabled activist because of the daily struggles that black disabled women have to undergo. Agreeing with Athena, she states,

I have often been asked which issue is more important to me: disablism, racism, sexism and so on. When I hear that I often feel that they don't have a clue what the real issues are for black disabled women, yet they are always trying to get us on their bandwagons by pretending to understand us and to speak on our behalf. All I do know is that as black disabled women, we have so many battles to fight we can't always be fighting all of them all of the time and having a healthy sex life as well.

Black disabled women are not one-dimensional and their sexual health cannot be boxed off from the rest of who they are. Raven summarised it by saying,

Before we can begin to address the subject of sexuality and sexual health for black disabled women we need first to be aware of the circumstances under which black disabled women are living. Our history, culture, economic status, male values, the influence of a predominantly white, male-dominated society and so many other things can all have an effect on our sexuality.

Family influences

With one exception, all the women interviewed felt that the family situations they were brought up in had influenced their sexuality. For the majority of them this was the reference point for their own sexual relationships. Many of the things learned in childhood can leave lifelong impressions. The family bonds of childhood memories and in particular the love/rivalry relationship between mother and daughter were central to most of the women's sexual identity. Regrettably, it was not always a positive point of reference.

Things my mother never told me

Just over 39 per cent of all the black disabled women who responded to the research (see Appendix 3, Fig. 29) said that they had had no positive role models in their childhood. This represents 3.8 per cent of the total. In addition, the majority of the women interviewed said that as far as they could recall their mothers had not been positive role models and they had received very little, if any, support regarding sexual issues; nor could any of them recall any supportive advice from their fathers. Ujima echoed the feelings of some of the women when she commented,

> Every now and again I will be doing something in relation to men or relationships and I will think, 'Oh God, I'm getting just like my mother and I definitely don't want to be like her,' but because I am my mother's daughter I seem to be repeating all her mistakes. She influenced the expression of my sexuality all right but it was only in a negative way.

Shona is in her mid-thirties and is a married woman with a young daughter. She was born into a large family and brought up mostly by what she describes as a strict but caring mother. She remembers that her mother never actually sat her down and told her 'the facts of life'. The little information that was given to her directly or that she was able to pick up from her family she remembers as being mostly negative. Shona always believed that this was because she had been born disabled and her family did not expect her to go on to have a sexual life. Shona says,

> I am working hard to try to be ready for my own daughter's sexual development when it comes. I am sure that this need to make sure that she feels good about herself and her sexuality is a direct result of the very negative feeling about my own sexuality that was given to me by my mother and my sisters. I don't know how much, if anything, my mother talked to my sisters about these things but I was always convinced that she didn't talk to me about them because I was disabled. I only wish that I had other disabled mothers with young children that I could talk to about these things.

Pat, who was also born disabled, is in her early fifties and is the mother of five girls. She feels that some difficulty she has in discussing sex and sexuality with her daughters has arisen because it was never discussed with her. Expressing similar sentiments to Shona, she says,

I got no sexual training or education from my family. I don't even remember getting any at school. It was something we just never talked about openly and I think that has carried over into my own life. At the age of seven I woke up to find my uncle and his wife making love. Even at that age I think I knew what it was but I don't know how I knew because sex was never discussed with me. As I was the only girl I don't know if it was because I was disabled but I do think that my family treated me differently because I was disabled.

In a similar vein Raven, who was born in 1951, explains,

The way I was brought up so many girls' and women's issues were not even open to discussion. It was not always heavy and repressive but the denial of all things feminine or to do with girls and women was always lingering in the background somewhere. If we were just watching television and the subject of abortion, or rape, or menstruation or just plain sex came up, my mother would immediately leave the room so there was no chance that we could discuss the issues with her.

Either that or she was very pre-emptive and would make some very cynical or jaded comment which would silence any question you felt you wanted to ask. I don't think it was peculiar to her as most of my friends' mothers at the time also dealt with the issues in that way. I think that it was learned behaviour because our own mothers' mothers had dealt with it similarly. I don't think disability had anything to do with it because I wasn't disabled at the time. She didn't talk to my sisters about it either – or to my brothers, for that matter. I just think that mothers of her generation didn't talk to their daughters about sexuality whether they were disabled or not.

Not-so-special school-days

The oppressive forces which create and sustain barriers to a full and healthy expression of black disabled women's sexuality would appear to be insidious at every stage of their lives. All of the women interviewed, even those who said that they had received no formal sex education at school, felt that their early education had had an imprint on their sexual development.

Racism in education

Sixty per cent of the women interviewed who went to school in Britain cited racism as a factor in their early development, though some felt that they had not recognised it for what it was at the time. However, upon reflection they had come to realise that racism and the inherent and often subtle repression of their racial, cultural and linguistic differences had had a negative influence on their self-esteem and self-confidence.

When assailed by so many negative myths and stereotypes about black women and black people generally, it was often difficult for some of them to maintain a positive sense of who they were. More than half of the women interviewed believed that they had internalised some of the negative imagery and messages that had been fed to them. At times in their lives they had even tried to live out the negative stereotypes. This, in turn, determined how and with whom they chose to explore their sexuality. Iman explains,

> *Throughout my school-days I experienced racism, whether it was from the teachers, my fellow students or other people somehow involved in my education. The racism was not always open and blunt but it was always there all the time. I remember that all the people in books were white, all the heroes in the books were white men, all the teachers were white. Everything was white, and on the odd occasion when we did talk about black women it was usually in the context of them being half-naked out in the African wilderness somewhere, having sex, sex, sex all the time, and carrying a whole lot of children swarming with flies that they couldn't feed or clothe or send to school because they had to work to support the younger ones.*
>
> *I didn't know it at the time because racism can be so indirect but all the while it was obscuring my sense of who and what I really was, so much so that I internalised a lot of what they were saying. Racism can really screw up your mind. I had that image of black women in my mind and I wanted to be as much unlike it as I could get. I am ashamed to say it now but for years I would only go out with white, usually non-disabled men. I swore that I would never have babies and made sure that I never did. Even as a black woman myself, the thought of going out with a black man was alien to me because I was always taught and, for a long time, believed that white was better. I am now living to regret much of my past behaviour and what I used to think about myself and my own people.*

Disablism in education

In addition to racism, disablism in education can also have a negative effect on black disabled women's self-esteem and sexuality. At least 70 per cent of the women I interviewed felt that they had experienced disablism while at school. Many of them felt that within that there was an element of negativity around disabled people's sexuality.

Liza is a single woman in her early thirties who feels that what she was taught about disabled people has had an influence on whom she selected as partners:

All of the men I have been out with have been able-bodied, and all of the men I have been out with have somehow wanted to collude with my not seeming blind. I am not exactly sure why that is or where it came from but I think that it must have something to do with what I was taught about disabled people. I didn't think about it much at the time. I was just so grateful to have someone going out with me. I now realise that I must have internalised a lot of negativity not only about being disabled but about being black as well, to the extent that even today I am still confused about a lot of issues and still have a lot of working out to do in my own mind.

Special-school education

All of the black disabled women in the study who had been born with impairments or who acquired them early in their lives were sent to special schools at some stage. There was general agreement among them that the education they received was substandard, inadequate, and did little to provide them with the skills necessary for adult living – much less for the development of a fulfilling sexual life. For example, nearly 47 per cent of respondents to the questionnaire (see Appendix 3, Fig. 28) stated that they wanted more information on sexual matters.

One of the interviewees who had been sent to special school typified the views of the others when she stated,

I think that my special-school education hindered not only my sex education but my general education as well. When I am around other people my age I feel so stupid because I was taught so little at school. I left school years ago and am still trying to catch up with courses and night classes. I think that special schools are a big mistake and unnecessary for a lot of disabled children who are sent to them.

More specifically, many of the women believed that the teaching in special schools perpetuates the false assumption that disabled girls and women are asexual or somehow sexually inadequate. Alex is a 31-year-old who was also sent to special school. She believes that she has a good understanding of her sexuality and is able to express it how she wishes. However, she feels that the sex education she received at school did little to help her come to that understanding. She explains,

At school the teachers did not let us explore and develop our sexuality as we thought our able-bodied friends were doing at [mainstream] school. I seem to recall that I was quite old before I was given any sex education by my teachers and

even then it wasn't very suitable because it taught me virtually nothing. And that was long after I had already developed sexual feelings and kissed my first 'boyfriend', which I remember made me feel really sick. My schooling wasn't that long ago but I don't imagine that things have changed much in special schools even today.

Iman is a 38-year-old who also attended special school. She has never married, although she says that she still has hope that one day she might. She feels that she denied her sexuality for many years and even today is shy about even talking about sex. Agreeing with Alex, she said,

Throughout all my years at special school the subject of sex was hardly ever talked about in the classroom and when the teacher did talk about it, it was always in a very cold and clinical way. As disabled students we were definitely made to feel that sex was not for us. We were therefore always very nervous about it and so didn't ask many question and learned very little.

Conventional and traditional

All of the women interviewed who acquired their impairments later in life naturally went to mainstream school. Of these, over 50 per cent said that they had received formal sex education at school. However, they felt that for the most part it reinforced the traditional concepts of gender stereotyping and sex roles. Gender equity or equality of the sexes was not present in their educational setting, and conventional attitudes, expectations and values were the substance of much of their formal education. None of them could recall much discussion about disability.

Raven is a wheelchair-user as a result of an accident when she was in her teens. She says,

I had finished primary school and had most of my secondary schooling behind me when I became disabled. Disability issues therefore played no part in my formative education although race and culture were very important at the time. I seem to recall that I received little, if any, sex education at school. I was educated to assume without question the traditional roles of wife and mother. I was educated under the traditional view of what girls were expected to do and what boys were expected to do. At my school we even referred to certain subjects as boys' subjects – such as chemistry and maths and certain subjects as girls' subjects – such as domestic science, English language and art.

Role change

The SHE research also shows that often if a girl is born disabled such traditional views about womanhood seem not to apply to her. For example, 36.46 per cent of all the women who responded to the research (see Appendix 3, Fig. 25) said that there was no expectation from their parents or teachers that they would go on to form sexual relationships or get married, while 65 per cent (see Appendix 3, Fig. 20) said that in childhood they had had those expectations of themselves. Moreover, it is often the case that should a single woman become disabled, her suitability for marriage and motherhood is then called into question.

Raven is in her early forties and one of the single women interviewed who spent her formative years in mainstream school, having acquired her disability in her early teens. She says,

> Ironically, once I became disabled it seemed that others no longer expected me to take up those traditional women's roles. In fact, I was positively discouraged from thinking about getting married and having children. I was told on a number of occasions that it would be unfair to ask any man to spend his life looking after me. I also felt that others thought that my expectations of myself must also have changed because I had become disabled.

Just good friends

Although formal education had for the most part failed the women in the survey, they all felt that their friends and peers at school had to some extent helped them in their sexual development. Alex explains,

> Most of what I learned about sex at school I learned from my classmates and friends. The teachers taught us next to nothing but when my friends and I used to get together during school times and holidays, the subject of sex always came up. I think we talked about it so much because we were being taught nothing about it in school. If it hadn't been for my friends, I would have come out of school knowing next to nothing about my sexuality.

Shardene is in her early twenties and believes that she still has a lot to learn about her sexuality. She feels that there are few people she can talk to about sexual matters and attributes her limited understanding to her lack of an adequate sex education while at school. She tells a similar story to Alex:

I learned most of what I know about my sexuality from my girlfriends at school, from my sister and from books and magazines, and I don't think that was much because I have had a lot of bad relationships and made a lot of mistakes through not knowing what to do. At school our teachers taught us hardly anything about sex. I think because we were disabled they didn't expect us to have a sex life. To tell the truth, they taught us hardly anything about anything at all. We used to go on outings a lot but I don't remember learning much about anything worth knowing about.

Culture and religion

Both the statistical evidence and that gathered during the interviews has shown that religion and culture have influenced the sexual identity of a significant number of black disabled women. For example, nearly 31 per cent of respondents (see Appendix 3, Fig. 31) said that their religion had had an impact on their sexual choices to some degree. Even among those black disabled women who said that their sexuality had not been influenced by religion, there was general agreement that religious practices and cultural beliefs are important features in many African, Asian and Caribbean communities.

In my sample there were women who were born in Britain, Africa, Asia and the Caribbean. Consequently, many different cultural, religious and ethnic identities were represented. Some of the women considered their cultural identity to be British, others that of the country where their parents or grandparents had been born. Yet more said that they straddled two or even more cultures in an effort to hold onto their separate identities within a host community where their 'own' cultures were not always readily accepted or accommodated. As a result, some beliefs and values varied from woman to woman even among those who claimed to come from the same cultural or religious tradition.

Cultural identity and sexuality

The study shows that 61 per cent of black disabled respondents (see Appendix 3, Fig. 32) highlighted ethnic origin as an issue for their sexuality. Moreover, a majority of these believed that their religion formed part of their culture and thus both culture and religion had had a lasting impact on their sexuality. Indeed, for some they were central to the manner in which they expressed it. At least 40 per cent of the interviewees said that their culture and religion had shaped and informed who and what they were and went to the heart of how they lived.

Some of the women said that they embraced this and readily allowed culture and religion to determine their sexual choices. However, others felt that they had in-built systems of monitoring and checking choices, lifestyles and life-chances which were unacceptable. For these women the rigours of many established cultural and religious practices proved to be a repressive force which could not easily accommodate their expression of sexual freedom.

For example, Pat is a practising Muslim who recently remarried. She explains,

> *My religion and cultural background say that women should be married before they start a sex life and that the woman's role within the marriage is to please her husband and family. Muslim women express themselves and find their sexual satisfaction and fulfilment through pleasing their husbands and their children and by making a good home. This may not be the view of all women who claim to be Muslims, but this is what I believe and I have no problems with it. Once you get married it doesn't matter whether you are disabled or not, the woman's role within marriage is to please her husband and family.*

Shona too believes that her religion determines her sexuality and how she conducts herself:

> *As a practising Christian, religion has always played an important part in my life, but most important of all was my love of children. I wanted to have a baby for years before I got married but because of my religious beliefs I would not have considered having one outside marriage because I was also taught that sex outside marriage was wrong. I even think that I only got married because I wanted a baby so much.*

Religion and culture had also had a profound influence on Fatima. A married mother of two young children, she felt constrained from even talking about her sexuality because of her religion. Like Pat, she is also a Muslim and concurs with her to some extent:

> *My religion teaches that a woman's sexuality is something which is private to her and her husband. Sexuality is not something that we are encouraged to discuss openly with others – not even with other women.*

Clash-point

By contrast, 40 per cent of the other women interviewed, although brought up within a religious setting, said that they had rejected religion to some extent as it clashed with how they wished to express their sexuality. They believed that female passivity was often an inherent feature in many traditional religious practices and argued that the historical repression of women in many religions did not allow for free expression of female sexuality. Thus the full equality of women and their sexual fulfilment and maturity were rarely addressed or accommodated within many religious and cultural contexts. For these women, their religion, and to some extent their culture, have proved to be the most constraining influence they have had to overcome when trying to achieve sexual enrichment and maturity.

When explaining why they had rejected their religion, several of the interviewees made references to the negative way in which women and disabled people are portrayed in many religious texts and teachings. As one of them stated,

> I was brought up in the church and I still think of myself as somewhat religious but the Bible is full of references to disabled people being unclean and possessed of the devil. In fact in my religion, the Christian religion, I am made to feel that my disability is a result of some awful sin that I must have committed, and if not me then most certainly one or both of my parents. As for women, I seem to recall that it says somewhere in the Bible that women should be followers of men and wherever the husband leads then the wife must follow. Well all I can say is 'bollocks' to that.

Raven was brought up in what she referred to as the strict Christian tradition. She described it as being like a noose around her neck slowly squeezing to death any expression of her individuality and sexuality:

> I felt that I had to reject so much of my religious upbringing before I felt free to explore my sexuality in the way that I wanted to because there were so many 'don'ts' for women within it. I remember that as a young girl I was frightened even to be seen talking to a boy alone for fear of getting into trouble. I was not allowed to wear jewellery or experiment with make-up or even go to dances or the cinema because it was considered sinful.

> In my Church women were conditioned to be subservient to men, especially their husbands, and accepting of anything that came along. It was all about getting

married and having children. I was taught so much God-fearing nonsense that the first time I entered into a sexual relationship I lay there afterwards and waited for God to strike me dead because I wasn't married. Even today I am haunted by it and whenever the least little thing goes wrong, I put it down to the fact that I have sinned against God and will suffer eternal damnation because I had sex outside marriage.

Sexuality and impairment

Although 40 per cent of the interviewees in this part of the survey were married or in long-standing sexual relationships, undoubtedly one's sexual health and well-being can be adversely affected by impairment and disability. In my sample there was a cross-section of impairments represented, including women with physical, sensory, learning and multiple disabilities. They all agreed that impairment and disability can often have an adverse effect on life chances and opportunities to explore sexuality. Physical, communication and, in particular, attitudinal barriers continue to operate in society to deny and limit the chances and choices of black disabled women.

No place to go

Ujima is a wheelchair-user who describes herself as a frustrated club goer and night owl. She explains,

I find that most of the places where people would usually go in order to socialise and make friends are inaccessible to me because I am in a wheelchair. The clubs and bars that my non-disabled friends go to are especially difficult as they are usually up or down lots of steps, and even if I can get in the loos, are always inaccessible, so either I don't drink when I am out, which is part of the reason why people go there, or after an hour or so I have to go home, which makes it not much point in wasting all that time and energy in going there in the first place, really. So I don't get to make friends and meet potential partners out in the wider community that often. I find that because of access problems most of my socialising is done within the disabled communities and the events that they hold, so my chances to meet potential partners are mostly restricted to disabled men, but I also find that people's attitudes also play a part in limiting my opportunities to socialise.

On those rare occasions when I do get out into the wider community on a social basis and I try to be 'friendly' with a man, I find his attitude quickly changes. It is almost as if they feel that disabled people shouldn't be doing things like that. They all seem to feel uncomfortable or frightened about a disabled woman giving them the 'come-on' because it might actually lead to something more and I think that really terrifies them – the idea of going to bed with a disabled woman.

At the other extreme, Raven described an experience shared by several women who said they had met non-disabled men who actually seek out the company of disabled women simply because they are disabled:

I have actually met men who have what I can only describe as a fetish for disabled women. They come up to you in public places or even in the street and tell you how much they admire you and how much they like disabled girls. I remember one came up to me at a party and actually started telling me about how he was going for counselling because he thought his attraction to disabled women was abnormal. Funnily enough, his counsellor thought so, too. Even I thought he was a bit weird because he kept on talking about how he liked having sex with disabled girls so much because he could put their legs where he wanted them. Sounded a bit like a control freak to me, so he was definitely in need of some kind of counselling, but I'm not exactly sure what for.

Lisa also expressed the opinion that impairment can limit disabled women's social interaction and opportunities to explore sexuality and to form personal relationships:

I feel, and people tell me, that I am not immediately perceived as being disabled in all circumstances. In those situations where my disability becomes irrelevant I think that my sexuality comes much more to the fore, but when my disability takes over I feel that the whole of my sexuality becomes reduced or is minimised.

Also, being visually impaired means that I find it difficult to meet potential partners because when I am in a party or social setting I can't see the men in the room so I don't know which one I might like to approach or whether or not I would wish to approach any of them. Physicality is a big part of it for me. If I could see I probably wouldn't have gone out with half the people I went out with. I also have trouble knowing if any man in the room is interested in me because I just can't see him.

Sexuality and relationships

More than 70 per cent of the women interviewed felt that there was still a widespread belief within the non-disabled communities that disabled women are asexual. However, all of the women in my survey were in or had been in a sexual relationship at some time. Moreover, all of them felt that in this couple-oriented society the natural order of things meant that women's expression of their sexuality automatically assumes that one should be in a permanent sexual relationship. Only Alex said that she had casual sexual partners:

> *I do have a few male friends who I can call to come over if I need to, but I think I am a romantic at heart, really, and so don't do that very often. I like all the things which go along with being in a relationship, such as the wining and dining, the friendship and companionship and just having someone to make you a cup of tea in the morning. They don't always sound important but those are the things that I miss when I am not in a relationship. Having casual sexual partners has its advantages but it is not the 'be-all-and-end-all'.*

Limiting choices

Although 61 per cent of black respondents (6.07 per cent of the total) (see Appendix 3, Fig. 32) said that their ethnic origin had influenced their sexuality, only 16 per cent felt that there was direct pressure on their individual sexual choices. With the exception of Lisa, who describes her sexuality as 'a bit of a grey area at the moment', all of the women described their sexuality as heterosexual. However, they all said that this was through natural inclination and not because of religious constraints or family or social pressures. Lisa, while acknowledging that there was still a widespread belief that disabled women are asexual, went on to say,

> *I personally don't believe that you need a partner in order to express your sexuality, but I appreciate the fact that this is not the accepted norm within society generally or within the black communities. I am also very conscious of the pressures within the black communities to be partnered and partnered with a black person and a black person of the opposite sex.*

> *I also feel that the pressure is on not just to have a partner but also to have a home and children and so on. As a consequence I find myself wishing that I had all those things, a partner whom I love and who loves me, a family and a home. In moments of wild optimism I can see light at the end of the tunnel and believe that one day it will happen. At other times I feel deep despair because I believe it won't, but that is what I want and also what everyone else wants and expects of me.*

Who's in control

Alex, a single mother, says that she likes being with a man and admits to having had a number of relationships. However, she believes that being in a relationship inevitably leads to the lowering of the woman's self-esteem:

Sooner or later power-play enters the relationship and leads to a loss of control for the woman. This seems to happen more if the woman is disabled. For example, even when I was having my son I did not feel I was in control. The doctors and the baby's father had taken all of the control completely away from me, even though I was the one who was having the baby. I think it is nice to be in a relationship but you have to be really strong not to allow the man to completely take over, and lots of disabled women have not been allowed to take control or learned how to be strong.

A fearful silence

Learning to deal with fears and difficulties in the sexual arena was an important issue for the women in this part of the survey. The sexual health of far too many disabled girls and women has been, and continues to be, blighted by serious and difficult issues. These may include sexual abuse, sexual dysfunction, abortion, and so much else that can erode or even destroy a woman's expression of her sexuality in a positive and rewarding way.

Even natural processes in a woman's development, such as menopause and ageing, are usually discussed with no reference to implications or issues related to disability. The women all agreed that there should be more encouragement and opportunity for black disabled women to discuss and resolve painful issues which touch and concern their sexuality and spiritual well-being. There was criticism of the fact that important issues for disabled women were continually swept under the carpet and not discussed because they were considered too difficult to deal with.

Disability and abuse

In particular, there was a great deal of concern that the sexual, physical and emotional abuse of disabled girls and women went largely unreported. Over 23 per cent of black disabled women responding to the questionnaires (see Appendix 3, Figs. 8–10) said that they had been abused, while 30 per cent of the interviewees testified to abuse of one form or another. They all believed that their impairments had contributed to the abuse and most said that they had received little, if any, suitable counselling for it. Consequently, significant numbers of disabled women have been living for years with frustration, pain and anger which they are unable to relieve.

Thus, in addition to the abuse, not being able to talk about it and resolve it can of itself have serious implications for women's sexual health. Ujima is the victim of years of physical, emotional and psychological abuse from members of her family. She stated,

> Because we are never given the chance to talk about these things, there is no chance that we can work through them and get them out of our system, so I and the disabled girls I know who have been abused have had to learn to deal with it all by ourselves, which isn't easy. I have to work really hard at not hating my family but every time I think of some of the things they did to me I would like to kill them.

Lisa was a victim of a sexual assault by a male family friend at the age of eight. She believes that many other disabled girls and women may have also been assaulted and abused but feel unable to speak about it or to relieve their pain precisely because there is such a veil of silence drawn over the issue. She explains,

> When I was eight a male family friend behaved towards me in a way which was wholly inappropriate and unacceptable. I didn't recognise it as abuse at the time but did have a real sense of shame as though I had done something really wrong, and what's worse I actually blamed myself for the incident having happened.
>
> I tried to push it to the back of my mind but it must have had an effect on me because years later when I saw the man again I was positively consumed by the same overwhelming sense of shame I had felt when the incident first took place. I was well into adulthood before I discussed it with another adult woman. It was only then that I recognised it as abuse and accepted the fact that it really wasn't my fault that it had happened. Talking it out was obviously very therapeutic. Of course, lots of disabled and non-disabled women who have been abused go on to have quite successful lives. They push it to the back of their minds and learn to cope, but why the hell should they have to?

Similarly, another of the women was the victim of rape when she was undertaking a further education course. She had never discussed it with anyone before so I have chosen not to refer to her even by her pseudonym. She said,

I have never talked about this to anyone before but I feel that it is important for this research because I am sure that there are other disabled women who are also living with dark secrets that they feel unable to tell people about. I feel that it might help them to know that they aren't the only ones that this has happened to.

She received no counselling after the incident and still today is fearful and apprehensive of any man she comes into contact with whom she perceives is of a background similar to that of the man who raped her. She recalls,

After I was abused I didn't talk to anyone about it because I didn't have anyone to talk to. I just put it to the back of my mind and learned to cope but even today I am afraid of all **** men, especially those who remind me of him. To this day, I always try to avoid being alone with any man or in situations where I know men like him might be.

I never talk much about things like this, I'm just not that kind of person, but I do think that there should be someone or some place where disabled women could go to talk about these things if they wanted to. I work a lot with other disabled women and I know by little things that they say every now and again that there are a lot of things that they would like to get off their chests if they could. It can't be doing them any good to keep it all bottled up all the time acting like it never happened. I know that it didn't do me any good.

Disability and sexual dysfunction

Sometimes disability and impairment can affect one's ability to 'perform' sexually. Of all the women who responded to the questionnaires, 45.3 per cent (see Appendix 3, Fig. 46) admitted to experiencing some sexual difficulties. For example, Ujima, a wheelchair-user as a result of spinal cord injury, says,

Although I have had a number of sexual partners, I have never had an orgasm. I am sure that this is because of my injury because I read somewhere that spinal injury can affect your sexual performance but I have never been told so by a doctor or anyone like that. Despite the fact that I don't have orgasms, I still like going to bed with men and do get a lot of sexual pleasure in other ways.

Anyway some men are so insensitive they don't know or care whether you are having an orgasm or not, or if they do ask, it is usually just to reassure themselves of their own manhood. Mostly I lie because if you do say 'no', they automatically assume that you are not normal, which only further complicates things because being disabled you're not considered normal in the first place. In fact, I often question myself about whether or not I am abnormal because I always thought

*that sex meant having orgasms, and I don't know where to go or even whom to go
to in order to find out about these things and whether or not anything can be done
about it.*

Many of the women in my study expressed the view that there is now an urgent
need for disabled women and representatives within the disabled communities
as a whole to begin to address some of these more important personal issues.
Continuing to ignore them and pretending that they are not happening
because they are considered too difficult to deal with is not benefiting disabled
women and may even be causing further disadvantage to them.

Blood sisters

A problem shared

Increasingly, gender identity and the issues which stem from it are coming
sharply into focus for black disabled women, but many feel that they need
support if they are to take more control over their sexuality and how they
choose to express it. For most this support will usually come from other black
disabled women. Finding strength and support through the sharing of common
experiences is fundamental to the process of sexual liberation.

Among the respondents there was some acknowledgement of the growing self-
help movement among black disabled women, the strengthening of black
disabled women's resolve, their politicisation and the celebration of their
dignity and self-respect. It was felt that these strengths should be used more to
help them to find resolutions to sexual health problems. Some called for the
establishment of a black disabled women's group through which to share
information, advice and positive experiences. They argued that only by
interacting and sharing information with other 'like minded' women could
they get the issue of black disabled women's sexuality on the agenda.

Throughout her lengthy interview, Liza was very open and frank with her
responses to all the questions, although she said that she rarely discussed sexual
matters with other disabled women. As she pointed out,

*I don't actually talk about the nitty-gritty of sex and other very personal matters
that much with anyone and when I do it tends to be with my non-disabled friends,
but I do think that there is a real need for support groups for black disabled women
and disabled women generally where we can get together to talk about sex and
sexuality and other things because for me women are where there is hope. I feel*

that some women engage much more with their emotional side and their intuitiveness. They take a much more holistic and sensitive approach to things that affect them.

Summary

Many black disabled women have long been aware of the notion of their own sexuality and its uniqueness. They demonstrate that they have assumed the responsibilities which result from the coming into being of a sexual consciousness. Black disabled women are asserting that the nature of their sexuality is no longer to be confused or distorted. Neither is the extent of it to be reduced or dismissed. They maintain that at this point in their historical and personal development others no longer have a role to play in defining or limiting their sexual identities or determining their priorities in this regard.

In spite of the many barriers put in their way, some black disabled women do go on to form successful sexual relationships and achieve a full and positive expression of their sexuality, but this should by no means understate how difficult it can be for many of them to do so. All of the women in my study were or had been in a sexual relationship at some time. Through the way in which they conduct their lives, they have begun to dismantle some of the barriers which hinder the full and free expression of their sexuality.

Anecdotal evidence will show that many others have not been successful in finding opportunities to express their sexuality. This is not always because these women do not have that expectation for themselves. It is more often the case that they simply find the many obstacles placed in the way of their progress too numerous and difficult to overcome.

The sexual health and equality hypotheses – Testing the hypotheses for black disabled women

1. That there is inadequate sex education for disabled women, particularly those who are born disabled

Of the black disabled women who responded to the questionnaires, 27 per cent stated that they had received little or no sex education (see Appendix 3, Fig. 2b). Of the interviewees, 60 per cent were born disabled or acquired their impairments in early life. Of these, 50 per cent said that they had received some sex education but most felt that it was inadequate and superficial.

2. That disabled women who acquired a disability later in life are more likely to be in a sexual relationship or have had sexual partners

Interview evidence provided the most detailed confirmation of this hypothesis. With one exception, 60 per cent of interviewees who were born disabled or who had acquired their impairments in early life all suggested that this had contributed to the difficulty they experienced in forming lasting relationships. Though 50 per cent of the women who had acquired their disabilities later in life were no longer in a sexual relationship, all said that they had been or had had sexual partners.

3. That race and/or religion influence sexual choices

The hypothesis that the race and religion of disabled women will influence their sexual choices and freedom to explore them proved to be definitive for black disabled women involved in this research. The most informative analysis of this hypothesis came from interview evidence, with 70 per cent stating that their religion had influenced their sexual choices and 60 per cent that their race had.

4. That a disabled woman's ability to express her sexuality is greatly influenced by her exposure, or lack thereof, to information about sexual choices

This was one of the hypotheses which proved more difficult for black disabled women to give an authoritative answer to. However, the most revealing insights came from interview evidence wherein 90 per cent of the women stated that they were heterosexual. All of them felt that this was through natural inclination though some acknowledged that there was often subtle pressure to explore their sexuality, through heterosexual relationships. However, they felt that this was due more to familial, societal and religious practices rather than to a lack of exposure to information about sexual choices.

5. That disabled women are more likely than non-disabled women to experience sexual and other abuse

This was yet another of the hypotheses which proved to be true for black disabled women, with 23 per cent of those who responded to the questionnaires stating that they had experienced sexual abuse. This is compared with a reported 20 per cent among the non-disabled populations. (Craft, 1994)

6. That disabled women lack positive role models to enhance self-esteem

This proved largely true for the black women who responded to the questionnaire survey, with only 22 per cent of them stating that they had had positive role models, while an overwhelming 38 per cent said that they had not. Interview evidence showed that this was a complex issue for black disabled women. They argued that there were still too few positive black role models whether male or female. This was further compounded by a lack of positive disabled role models.

7. That disabled women do not practise safer sex

The questionnaire answers given to this hypothesis were not conclusive either way, with 50 per cent of black disabled women (6.07 per cent of respondents) stating that they practised safer sex (see Appendix 3, Fig. 30). Of those who were interviewed, 60 per cent said that they did not practise safer sex but that this was because they were either married or not in a sexual relationship.

8. That disabled women are reluctant to talk to each other about sex, but will talk to others about it

In testing this hypothesis, the survey was inconclusive, with 47 per cent of black disabled women who responded to the questionnaires stating that they are reluctant to talk to other disabled women about sex but will talk to others about it. The interview evidence produced similar findings with 45 per cent of the interviewees saying that they rarely discussed sex with other disabled women. However, many of them said that it very much depended on the circumstances. They felt that sex wasn't talked about among black disabled women because there were so few opportunities for them to get together in order to do so.

I shall call you
(for the purposes of this piece
as they say)
Fiona.

I count myself unfortunate –
friendships don't come easy to me
and you are a list, Fiona,
depressingly long,
of people I had trusted
were my friends.

It is hard, now,
to remember this –
that you were my friends, Fiona –
but, for the purposes of this piece,
we all must.

Dear Fiona,

> *You treat me*
> *like a disease*
> *a horrifying abnormality*
> *as sad*
> *as a threat*
> *as sick*
> *frightening*
> *disgusting*
> *as deliciously right-on*
> *an alternative lifestyle*
> *as someone you could name-drop about*
> *('some of my best friends are …')*
> *and then, whenever you liked,*
> *drop*
> *in the shit*

There were three main types of symptoms among you Fiona –
Although some of you, disturbingly, displayed them all.
Fiona Type 1
withdrew
disgusted/shocked/frightened
and that hurt
with the appalling pain of bewilderment
and betrayal of trust.

I screamed for acceptance … tolerance … liberalism
I denied I was a threat
I worked hard – 24 hours a day –
to be a shining ambassador
of normality
– the NORMAL lesbian.

Fiona Type 2
displayed intense disinterest,
extreme right-on-ness
and came out with things like:

'It doesn't make any difference to me'
'You're still the same person'
'You mustn't let it change you'
'Well, I don't think you look like one'

It was all really positive stuff.

Fiona Type 3
started standing too close to me
making excuses to touch me
with schoolgirl giggles
I had never heard from her before
while she loudly proclaimed
her two-children-and-happily-married bliss.

This
forced hot and acrid bile
into my throat
for in these cases, Fiona,
it was your turn to disgust me.

It was with this taste in my mouth
that I gradually weaned myself away
from trying to be the most perfect
and balanced
thoroughly nice human being who-just-happened-to-be-a-lesbian.

And it was with the sweet, salty taste
of woman
in my mouth
and wondrous, revolutionary ideas
blasting around my heart and head
that I wrapped myself
in our community
replenished my depleted larder
with truer friends.

Char March

Chapter 2

Women loving women

Issues for disabled lesbians and bisexual women

This section is based on the responses of the 45 disabled lesbians and bisexual women who responded to the SHE questionnaire, and on the testimonies of 20 women who were interviewed by the lesbian researcher or submitted written statements about their experiences as disabled lesbians or disabled bisexual women.

The same old prejudices!

While there are obvious differences in the experiences of disabled lesbians and bisexual disabled women, i.e. lifestyle, identity and the particular experience of prejudice that comes from these women's apparent 'rejection' of men in a patriarchal society, it would appear that many disabled lesbians and bisexual women share the same concerns as their heterosexual sisters. They are not considered worthy partners, lovers, home-makers or mothers. Due to sub-standard education, or enforced unemployment following disablement, many women were denied the opportunity of a career and economic independence, which would have been a realistic alternative to dependence on family or carers. The best they could do was to attempt to find a place for themselves in a society that does not value them. The 'choices' were often at great personal cost to themselves. Many disabled women felt they could not compete with the 'acceptable' face of femininity, or live according to rigid gender roles. They felt they were perceived as inferior, second-rate, flawed females, who were all too readily available for marriage or sex *as damaged goods*.

Inadequate role models

Of the disabled women in the study, 54.14 per cent did not have positive role models and therefore felt excluded from mainstream, or as one respondent put it, 'malestream' society (see Appendix 3, Fig. 15). They felt that the reality of their lives was not reflected in magazines, papers, TV, radio or film. They felt alienated from the commonly recurring stereotypes of disabled women. All too often the media depict disabled people as wheelchair-users, probably for simplicity; however, the majority are not wheelchair-users and can feel excluded by such representation. As Julie, a mental health system survivor, states,

> *If somebody is depicted as 'disabled' they are more commonly pictured in a wheelchair. I suppose 'hidden' disabilities are nigh impossible to portray. Images of us are generally dismal, uncool, not sexually appealing and completely lacking in adventure and stimulus. These images are a sexual turn-off and a complete blow to the confidence.*

Brenda states that the world sees disabled women as 'ugly, grey, unfashionable, boring and stupid'. She adds,

> *You certainly wouldn't want to be disabled or be friends with us! Being disabled sets us apart and I hate it. I think these views are wrong but are largely due to segregation, particularly in education.*

The other major way disabled women are perceived by the media is as 'super-cripples'. This is also alienating, as it is unrealistic and unrepresentative. Brenda explains,

> *I hate seeing disabled people bungee-jumping in wheelchairs and similar stuff. It's unrealistic and aping able-bodied people, which we are not.*

Even when we have 'specialist' programmes that are supposed to represent us, such as Channel 4's *Dyke TV*, we are rarely visible as disabled lesbians. There has been a 'flood' of lesbians in 'soaps' on TV, but again they are glamorous, gorgeous 'babes', or 'lipstick lesbians' as younger, fashion-conscious lesbians are currently called. The representation of lesbians on TV is generally through an image unattainable by most disabled lesbians. It would appear that even the lesbian community has bought the 'body beautiful' youth culture of the 1990s. 'You only have to go to a disco to realise to what extent lesbians have bought the idea of the slim, agile, symmetrical body.'(Hearn 1988)

Pat states,

> *Lots of people aspire to the 'body beautiful' and it can and does make those of us who are not and will not fit in, feel uncomfortable and unconfident about our self-images. My body is beautiful because I exist, not because my skin is smooth, unscarred, so glamorous.*

When disabled women sought positive images or role models which they could identify with, there was none to be found. Those disabled people who make it to the TV screen, are either super-beings, abseiling in wheelchairs for charity or the courageous victims of fate who have 'overcome' the tragedy of disability as depicted in 'Children in Need'-type jamborees. However, more commonly presented are the stereotypical, bitter and twisted 'cripples', whose lives are a burden to themselves and others. Most women were aware of the predominant images of disabled women as pathetic, tragic, needy, dependent, asexual or unsexy, childlike, boring and unattractive.

Most lesbians and bisexual women interviewed had adopted a view of themselves that they presented to the world which was a more confident, capable, coping and sometimes 'shocking' representation, to challenge these negative stereotypes. Sara explains her way of dealing with people's expectations of her:

> I dress however I want, in leather or rubber. People are often shocked as it's unexpected. I also deny help if I can manage, upsetting people's ideas of how I should be. This way I keep my independence and power.

Zora's reaction to these stereotypes and negative images is to ridicule them in her work as a cartoonist. She says,

> My cartoons have helped me a lot to deal with the usual daily comments of people, such as 'What happened to you then?' I would like to come across as competent and efficient in what I do and creative and talented. This is more important than whether I am seen as 'sexy' or beautiful. I would like to dress better but as a fat crip on a low income, it ain't easy. As a woman I certainly don't fit into the feminine role and have never wanted to. I would rather be dead.

The absence of positive role models and the impact of negative stereotypes cannot be underestimated as an important factor in the erosion of disabled women's self-esteem.

Thus, disabled lesbians and bisexual women would appear to have no role models with whom they can identify to validate their experience, or to challenge the idea that they are freaks of nature or deviant women. As one respondent said,

> I thought I was the only blind lesbian in the world.

However, in response to this absence of positive images, or accurate representation, many disabled lesbians and bisexual women have fought back. They have involved themselves in the struggle for political change with considerable success and in doing so, have become role models for younger or newly disabled women. The research found that 44 per cent of lesbians (6.08 per cent of respondents) and 25 per cent of bisexual women (2.76 per cent of respondents) (see Appendix 3, Fig. 15) stated they had positive role models, but at interview these role models were other disabled lesbians or bisexual women who had been supportive during the process of their 'coming out' as lesbians, bisexual or disabled women.

Inadequate sex education

Of all the women in the study 42.54 per cent received no sex education at all (see Appendix 3, Fig. 2). Of those disabled women who attended special school, 42.54 per cent did not receive sex education (see Appendix 3, Fig. 27). The general impression was that sex was for others and although this may not have been stated outright or openly, young disabled women 'understood' that sex was not for them. Those who attended mainstream schools may have been denied sex education for religious reasons, or due to pressure from the family. As Dorothy explained,

> *Any subject around sex or sexuality was completely taboo. We had one lesson on menstruation, and that was it!*

Those who did receive sex education found it limited. As Jo explained,

> *It was all about heterosexuals and based around reproduction.*

However, many lesbians and bisexual women know a great deal about sex education and safer sex, as a result of the impact of the human immunodeficiency virus (HIV) and acquired immune deficiency syndrome (AIDS) on the lesbian and gay community. The research revealed that 40 per cent of lesbians (6.62 per cent of respondents) and 35 per cent of bisexual women (4.42 per cent of respondents) practised safer sex (see Appendix 3, Fig. 14), but at interview the awareness of HIV and AIDS was particularly high and their involvement was considerable.

In particular disabled lesbians, like their non-disabled sisters, have become involved in providing information and services to people living with AIDS. Information is available in the gay press, or from HIV/AIDS agencies such as the Terrence Higgins Trust or Positively Women. Although this may not always be in the format needed (e.g. tape, Braille or large print), there is a growing awareness that information in other formats is not a luxury and may just save lives. There is also more discussion among lesbians about HIV, because so many know someone, or have loved someone infected by the virus. As Sara states,

> *I had one disabled girlfriend who had AIDS. She eventually died of it. I worked at the Terrence Higgins Trust as a counsellor so I know a great deal about sex education.*

HIV and AIDS are increasingly becoming an issue in the disability community, as the virus begins to have an impact on particular impairment groups. This is largely due to the lack of accessible, relevant information. Kay describes a sex education workshop for people with learning difficulties:

> It had come to light in a particular London borough that men and women with learning difficulties were having sex. They were in heterosexual and gay relationships and the staff were unsure what to do about it, if anything. It was decided that a policy was needed as a guidance document. Following a considerable consultation period, I held a workshop with 20 people with learning difficulties. They opened up to me because, as a wheelchair-user, I couldn't possibly be a staff member, so I was probably more like themselves. Although three of them had been married, one re-married and others were sexually active, none of them had had any sex education and were obviously confused about contraception and safe sex. It was commonly thought that the Pill, injections or sterilisation protected them from HIV. Thankfully, a lot of work has been done with these disabled people since then, but I'm sure this was not an isolated incidence.

Thus disabled people are becoming advocates to people living with HIV and AIDS because they are familiar with services and systems and how they work. Along with an increased awareness of HIV and AIDS, disabled lesbians appeared to have considered the implications of safer sex for themselves; 48 per cent of disabled lesbians stated that they practised safer sex (see Appendix 3, Fig. 14), as opposed to only 34 per cent of heterosexual women and 35 per cent of bisexual disabled women. These statistics are alarming as they indicate that disabled women are having unprotected sex and putting themselves at risk of contracting sexually transmitted diseases, including HIV. The actual percentage of lesbians practising safer sex is probably higher than 40 per cent as the 'no' and 'not applicable' responses may represent lesbians who do not engage in sexual activity that carries a risk of sexually transmitted disease, including HIV.

This is a significant change from the initial viewpoint that lesbians were not at any risk from the virus. One disabled lesbian stated that she definitely would not have sex with a lover while she was menstruating. Most disabled lesbians and bisexual women had heard of dental dams or other forms of protection, but some women, especially those living in rural areas, did not know how to obtain them. Others had considered the use of dental dams and latex gloves and, as sex was rarely spontaneous – for a number of practical reasons apart from impairment (unlike gay men, lesbians do not go 'cottaging', and rarely have sexual encounters in public places) – the use of such protection could be planned.

Sexual health services

Generally the sexual health services are designed for non-disabled women. In addition to access difficulties, the attitudes of staff are often problematic. This apart, being presented with a waiting room of young 'normal' women can be daunting. Lesbians are often thought not to need these services. However, some lesbians have had heterosexual relationships in the past or are currently having sexual relationships with men, but still regard themselves as lesbians. Bisexual women also require regular cervical screening and breast examination, services offered at well-woman clinics but all too often not accessible to disabled women. Of the lesbians interviewed, 30 per cent have children by previous heterosexual relationships or via donor-insemination and require periodic cervical screening. There are also women who are in abusive situations, where they are coerced or actually forced into sexual activity. These women would benefit from regular physical examinations and referral to counselling and advice agencies. However, these services are often not accessible to disabled women, or women feel they are not appropriate services that they can use.

Many women felt that their only recourse was to their GPs, and they were not always comfortable with disability or lesbianism. Dorothy explains how her GP, although pleasant enough, spent most of the consultation talking about and to her guide dog and did not tackle her problem:

> I eventually went to a GUM clinic and saw a really nice woman doctor four or five times and I was sorted. I even allowed her to do a smear. She was so gentle, whereas smears at the surgery were horrendous.

Although the responses to the questionnaire demonstrate that most disabled women in the study do *not* practise safer sex (38.1 per cent, including 'sometimes') (see Appendix 3, Fig. 14) and some responses suggest confusion between safer sex and contraception, this is not surprising, given the dearth of information about sexual health available to disabled women. Even those women contemplating sexual relationships or motherhood had little choice other than to go to their GPs for information, advice and treatment. GPs and primary health care staff vary enormously in their attitude to disabled women's sexuality and in the services they offer. While some disabled women find these services acceptable, others believe that doctors are not the best people to give advice about sexual matters and in fact can impose their prejudicial views. As Bridie states,

> *It is hard to explain to a doctor who is not aware of one's sexuality, why it really is so important to strengthen limbs and achieve pain control, so that one can enjoy being sexual.*

Disabled women firmly believe that they should have the same range of services available to them as non-disabled women (e.g. sexually transmitted disease (STD) or genito-urinary medicine (GUM) clinics, family planning clinics, infertility and donor-insemination services). Jenny explains,

> *Some doctors have been insensitive but generally the services have been OK. However, I think it is important to have our own health care services, like the Sandra Bernhardt Clinic where it is assumed we are lesbians and it's no big deal or embarrassment. We need to be able to choose.*

The impact of religion/culture on sexual expression and choices

Of women from minority ethnic communities, 37.02 per cent (see Appendix 3, Fig. 32) stated that their ethnicity influenced their sexual identity, and 30.1 per cent stated that religion influenced their sexual choices (see Appendix 3, Fig. 31). Thus the woman's ethnicity, culture and/or religion may have an impact on her ability to express her sexuality. Gloria, raised in a Catholic family within a Catholic community, was unable to consider anything other than heterosexuality despite her most deep-seated feelings. Gloria explains why Catholicism limited her choices:

> *My gut instincts told me I could not love any man. The culture I grew up in (close Scots Catholic community) did not allow me to think about women. If I could not love any man, I could find someone who I would be happy to live with, and my criterion for someone to marry then was a man who didn't drink! I was terrified of having a drunken man in the house. When I found that man who didn't drink, I was aware I never loved him, but it would work ... Look at what we do to ourselves!!*

Sara talks about pressures from her Catholic community:

I had my first lesbian relationship at the age of ten but I was severely punished by the Irish Catholic community in which I lived. I was asexual from 10 to 19. I tried to be heterosexual, as this was expected of me. When I was 19 I married and had three children. I became unhappy and left my husband to be with a woman.

Kay explains that she was actively lesbian when she was 13 but at 16 she was forced to go out with boyfriends and eventually marry:

I always knew I loved women and even when I was persuaded to go with men, most of my fantasies were about women. My family were devout Irish Catholics and I was expected to marry and have children. Sex outside marriage was a 'mortal' sin so I married only having had sex with women. Although I believed I loved my husband and loved him as the father of our children, I soon discovered what a great mistake I had made. I never enjoyed sex but was told by my GP to get on with it, as most women didn't like it anyway. After ten years and two children later I nearly went mad. I had to leave the home I'd built and the family I loved, to start a new life with nothing, just to be myself! Religion and cultural pressures have a lot to answer for.

Sexual identity

As the testimonies demonstrate, it has taken disabled women many years to achieve a sexual identity that most non-disabled women take for granted in their early teens. Growing up with an impairment has often meant a denial of sexual feelings by parents or care-givers. Messages that their status as asexual is the only one acceptable require great inner strength to reject, especially as these messages come from those providing essential care and 'love'. At times when sexual feelings are particularly strong and should be celebrated as a sign of healthy growth, disabled young women may have their feelings rejected as inappropriate. Women may take years to recover, or may not recover at all, from such damaging rejection. As Barbara explains,

My particular experience is that I had my sexuality forbidden/crushed out of me just as it was beginning to emerge in my mid-teens. For the last five years I have been struggling to reclaim it.

Those women who had a strong sense of their sexual identity, may still have found that expressing their sexual feelings was too risky. Concerns about body image and fears of rejection, in a society that is dominated by images of perfect bodies, add to women's isolation and chastity or enforced celibacy. As Liz states,

My disability is at the forefront at all times and in all ways. I can't go places to meet people, so my experience is limited. I think few, if any, people ever think of me as a sexual being.

Those women whose sexual identity is lesbian or bisexual may need to hide the fact. As Ruth states,

I can talk about being heterosexual but not bisexual because that is not acceptable and I don't feel confident or safe.

The reaction of family, religion or culture to women's sexuality may keep them in 'unhappy' marriages, chaste or single. For some women, adopting another 'negative' label may take some getting used to. Gloria explains the effect of messages she was given as a disabled child:

I had so many negative messages from using a wheelchair as a child … where the only divisions were Catholic or non-Catholic and all the children wore uniforms except the disabled children who were bussed to school. So to leave all that behind and be one of the crowd …

Having spent so much energy hiding a 'disabled' identity because of the negative stigma, the idea of identifying with another oppression was too difficult to cope with for some time. However, after much soul-searching and a very positive sexual experience with a woman, Gloria has 'come out' as disabled and lesbian:

I've spent so much time putting my disabled identity aside to be a lesbian and now I can have both!

Disabled lesbians and bisexual women felt they were particularly invisible as a minority within a minority, in a society where disability and sexuality are still a major taboo. They present society with an uncomfortable dilemma, in stating that they are both disabled and sexual and that their sexual expression is towards other women.

Women in the study stated that they were not expected to grow up and be sexual partners, wives or mothers: 36.46 per cent (see Appendix 3, Fig. 25) stated that their parents or teachers had no expectation of them forming sexual relationships or getting married. They were not considered to be potential partners and were not expected to have active sex lives.

Some women felt that not having the usual expectations of wife and mother enabled them to express their true sexuality as lesbians. One woman described how, before her accident, she was expected to marry and have children. However, following her injury all those pressures disappeared, and she was able to get involved with a woman and she and her lesbian lover passed as 'friends'. They experienced a freedom which comes from removal of social norms.

There is an element of conflict between lesbians and bisexual women as lesbians are commonly subject to ridicule and violence because of their perceived total rejection of men. One woman stated that it is hard to convey the depth of oppression experienced by lesbians in our society. It is even more complicated for disabled lesbians who may be even more vulnerable. Dorothy explains,

> We all know that having good access to public transport is vital but my partner and I dare not travel on public transport because I have no choice but to link arms with her. Because our appearance identifies us as lesbians, we feel very threatened and until now we have only been verbally abused. It is the same for us when we walk in the street. If I were a sighted woman, although we would suffer harassment and oppression, it would be quite different.

Coming out as lesbian, bisexual and/or disabled

There appear to be similarities between 'coming out' as disabled and coming out as a lesbian or bisexual. Although some women could pass as non-disabled, most women in the study had obvious impairments which meant they were immediately identifiable as disabled women, their physical appearance 'outing' them as disabled. However, many disabled women felt that 'coming out' as a lesbian was a matter of choice which depended upon support, time and place and their relationships with family and carers. Some women described a powerful change in themselves when they identified as 'disabled' or 'lesbian'. This change had arisen out of an understanding of their position in society, a process of politicisation and a shared experience and identity with others like themselves. As Kay states,

> I had worked through the issues of coming out as a lesbian and although it was at great personal cost, I had to be true to myself. Attending women's groups and listening and talking to other lesbians made it possible. When I became disabled, the process I went through seemed so familiar, dealing with other people's prejudices and assumptions about who I was, or what I was capable of. I joined a disabled women's group called Sisters Against Disablement, where I learned how

to deal with the oppressive way disabled women, and in particular disabled lesbians, are treated in our society. I can't describe the importance of being with other women like myself.

Some women lived with an impairment for many years without identifying as a disabled person. Gloria had such negative feedback about being disabled that she hid it and passed as non-disabled whenever possible. It is only in the last few years that she has changed her ideas about disability and now identifies in a positive way. She explains,

The process of coming out as a disabled woman happened just last year ... 42 years later.

When that positive identification took place women were able to make connections with other oppressed groups, understand long-standing confusing feelings, seek support and work towards personal empowerment. Paula explains,

I lived with my 'illness' for many years before identifying as a disabled person. I thought I was the only disabled person in the world, I felt angry and didn't know why. As far as my sexuality was concerned I assumed it was all over.

Paula describes her first meeting with other disabled people:

I felt shit-scared. I was sitting in this room with disabled people and I'd not done this before. Lots of things went through my mind, like, 'Should I really be here, is this giving up, will I be accepted?' But I also felt excited and alive at the outrage and anger that were being expressed. I knew this was it: I belonged.

Gill explains how having a political identity as a disabled person made it easier to come out as a lesbian when she subsequently found herself in love with a woman:

I didn't identify as a lesbian initially, I just happened to be a woman who was in love with another woman.

However, being around politicised disabled people made it easier to identify with the political aspects of being a lesbian. Some lesbians are not able to be open about their sexual identity in every area of their lives. Some women feel it is not yet safe for them to be out as disabled lesbians in their places of work or feel they have too much to lose coming out to their families. Gill says,

I feel that in most of my working environment, which is around other disabled people, to be out as a disabled lesbian is impossible. It seems too much for people to cope with and I feel too vulnerable at this time.

Dorothy explains how her lesbianism is viewed by her family and friends:

After an abusive relationship with a man, I got to grips with my lesbian identity, which had been suppressed for many a long year. My family feel threatened by my sexuality and the fact that I have independence now means that they cannot contain me and control me any longer. Most of my family and heterosexual 'friends' don't speak to me any more. This makes me feel quite alone at times and vulnerable.

Kirsten states,

I came out as disabled in 1981 and out as a lesbian in 1982 and I think without the one, there may not have been the other. I might have been wandering around in this hideous heterosexual miserable life not owning up to who I was as a disabled person, not being able to say it's not my problem. In the same way I may not have been able to say anything about my sexuality, so I see that those are very strong connections.

Other women have had to overcome the prejudice and anti-lesbianism of family and professional helpers, whose prejudice has contributed to their distress. Gloria explains,

Coming out as a lesbian was all about feelings, about me thinking about my sexuality, and did I want to be part of a minority group who were terribly oppressed, as I had spent a large part of my life being part of a minority group who were terribly oppressed? Did I want to do this again? Was it worth it? I did not know. I wasn't in a sexual relationship with a woman; this was head space I was in. I felt happy with women, but was this worth being the outcast in society, standing up and being different? How do I introduce this woman to people as 'my friend'? All this thinking took about two years. My therapist spoke out against my decision, the only time she passed judgement, but it put me back six months. She said I should make the effort and struggle on but the more I thought about it the more alien it felt. I thought of living my life in celibacy with no label.

Lesbianism is often seen as a second-rate, lesser choice than heterosexuality. It is assumed that disabled women cannot attract men, and have therefore turned to women. As Ann explains,

> *I did all that (dating men and having heterosexual relationships) before my accident. I always knew I was a lesbian, having crushes on older girls at school, but my mum is my best friend and I didn't want to lose that. Not being able to be out as a lesbian was more painful than being paralysed. However, when I told my mum, she was great about it. She could see the transformation in me, how happy I was and she was happy for me. My parents are so supportive and don't interfere. My girlfriend can't believe how lucky I am because her family are quite homophobic really.*

On the other hand, many women identified as lesbians before they acquired a disability and had actively chosen lesbianism over heterosexuality. These women viewed their lesbianism as more a way of living than a sexual preference, a lifestyle that prioritises women in a patriarchal society. For many lesbians this political analysis of their position in society made their identification as disabled women so much easier. Ruth had been active within the women's and lesbian communities as a lesbian feminist for many years:

> *As a lesbian I had issues of exclusion as a mother, so the progression to being disabled was not that kind of incredible shock. It was more of the same.*

For some women, discovering their lesbianism has been really liberating. They have had to overcome the fear of living with two forms of oppression but have ultimately opted to be true to their feelings. Gloria explains,

> *I met this woman and I felt the same way for her as I had been taught to feel for a man. I found it a funny feeling and I knew I wanted more but I wasn't sure what that more consisted of. The feelings got stronger and she was the woman I had my first lesbian relationship with. That was such a wonderful, positive experience, it was such a celebration of her body. It was so wonderful, so familiar, that it made me realise this is what I should have done 20 years ago.*

Lois states,

> *I'm convinced that a sexual identity is absolutely vital to any sense of self-esteem, and must be fought for from the idea that in order for adults to be 'adult' they have the right to be acknowledged as sexually active individuals.*

Sexual function

Those lesbians and bisexual women who overcome the inherent difficulties in being a disabled woman and go on to form sexual relationships or meet lovers may have additional 'practical' problems to overcome. Of the women in the study, 68 per cent of the lesbians and 50 per cent of the bisexual women (see Appendix 3, Fig. 46) stated that sex was difficult due to physical problems. As Gill said,

Sex can be difficult because I am in constant pain and cannot lie on my right side. I have loss of and altered sensation all down my right side. I have been rejected because people can't be bothered to take the extra effort needed to overcome my difficulties.

Bridie explains that following a whiplash injury sex became less fun and was at times painful. As she was unable to assume certain positions she felt unsure of herself and worried that things felt different for her partner. Bridie explains,

I had less power in my arm and hand and at times it was very painful to make love to my partner and my partner became less inclined to make love to me for fear of hurting me.

Julie explains how her medication affects her sexual function:

Sometimes the medication I am on causes me to dry up I use 'sex grease' or 'probe' and that solves the problem. Apart from making me dry my medication means I am easily tired and can feel vulnerable. I feel able to discuss this with my current partner but it's been a sensitive area with lovers in the past.

Liz is extremely isolated and cannot get out to meet partners. She explains,

I know I'm sexy and need sex but never get it. The only sex I've had for 30 years has been with a vibrator or before that with my hands.

Morgan, who is deaf and uses sign language, explains,

Communicating about sex and during sex can be difficult if the other person doesn't sign.

Ruth describes the feelings of frustration in having to concentrate on overcoming difficulties in day-to-day living as a disabled woman who needs personal assistance:

Given how difficult it is to get the basic support, where just getting out of the house or going to the pictures is such a luxury, having a discussion with your care

manager about whether they can provide you with the gizmos to be able to have sex seems bizarre. Realistically you would probably be told it was your responsibility or your lover's. I think it is about overcoming the embarrassment of talking about sex. I think people find it one of the most difficult things because most of us, to varying degrees, are embarrassed by our bodies.

Changes in Zora's body size and function have affected her sexual activity:

I used to be a lot more mobile generally and I miss this. There are few positions I can now use: my hand gets tired easily, and I cannot kneel, which I find quite restrictive. Also I am a lot more fat since I have become disabled – both this and my knee impairment mean I cannot lie on top of my lover as I wish to.

Jenny explains how needing to wear a spinal jacket can limit her sexual freedom:

I would like to be able to react in any situation, to do what comes naturally or spontaneously. If I want my breasts touched I would like my lover to do that without having to think about it and prepare for it.

Ann explains how, after she became paralysed, she could find no information about sex that was of any use to her; what was available was for paralysed men. She had to find out for herself by experimenting. Now, a few relationships later, she knows exactly what turns her on.

My neck is my clitoris and my shoulders are my 'G spot'. I don't have to feel my body to get off on watching my girlfriend touching the numb parts of me.

There are obvious practical problems for many disabled lesbians and bisexual women as a result of their individual impairments and the lack of appropriate sources of help. They also have to cope with the often unwelcoming and hostile lesbian and gay community, which appears embarrassed and confused by its disabled members. However, there are certain pleasures in having to be creative about sexual practice. As Kay explains,

I spent a lot of energy worrying over which side to strap the catheter and, even before that, whether my partner could even cope with the idea of this tube in the way. However, as things have progressed and I have become more numb and less able to feel her touch, we have had to work hard at finding other ways to turn me on. What started as a serious endeavour has had us in fits of laughter on many occasions and on a recent trip to the States we popped into a sex shop for a quick look and spent two days playing with a vibrator, dildos and a whole host of sex toys. Thank God we didn't get stopped at customs! We are still experimenting with the toys. Making love has become much more visual, along with a good line in erotic fantasy, and we have more magic. I often wonder if we would still be bothering to find out what works sexually if we hadn't had to because of my impairment.

Bridie is also having to try things differently in order to remain sexually active:

Currently I cannot squat, kneel or bend and this has meant being a little creative in bed and adopting positions which do not hurt.

Lois explains,

To be honest I think sex with a disabled man or woman is in many cases more interesting than with able-bodied people. It can be a bit of a relief to be with somebody whom you don't need to educate ethically.

Opportunities to socialise and meet potential partners

As a result of the segregated, often second-class education received by disabled children and the consequent lack of educational or vocational qualifications, disabled people are often unprepared for the workforce. This, compounded by discrimination on the part of employers, means that most disabled people are not in paid work, are living at home, or in 'caring' situations, relying financially on state benefits. Work provides not only an important place for people to meet potential partners, but also the financial means necessary to socialise.

Lack of access to social events means that many disabled women do not develop the social skills or confidence necessary to meet friends or potential partners. Most of the disabled lesbians and bisexual women interviewed complained about the lack of access and negative attitudes in the lesbian and gay scene. Although 'community' groups, such as Lesbian Line or Lesbian Avengers, were generally more aware and welcoming, most disabled lesbians and bisexual women felt alienated by the 'body fascism' that exists within the lesbian culture of the 1990s. Ruth says,

I feel irritated and alienated by the gay scene. I don't go to clubs as I can't breathe or hear and I often can't get in the clubs in the first place.

Pat explains,

> *Venues and attitudes have made access difficult. However, I have a good support network, which means I am not always the one to bring up these issues.*

For those disabled lesbians living in rural communities there is the additional problem of few or no lesbian or gay venues in which to meet others. There may be pubs or clubs that have a 'gay night' once a month, but these are often sited in larger towns and transport and access remain problematic. Thus opportunities to meet and socialise with other disabled lesbians are even fewer than for those in urban areas and the isolation can be intolerable. Disabled lesbians or bisexual women in these settings often have to rely on contact advertisements in the lesbian and gay press or settle for 'penpals' if opportunities to meet are impossible.

Most major cities and some large towns have Lesbian Lines and/or Gay Switchboards offering information, support and advice to lesbian or bisexual callers. However, many of these services have little awareness of the needs and requirements of disabled members of the community, and it is extremely rare for such services to hold information about venues which are accessible and/or disabled- and lesbian-friendly. Of the women in the study who sought help about problems, about 16 per cent (see Appendix 3, Fig. 13 (iii)) said the help was not appropriate to them as disabled women. After working with Spinal Injuries Scotland, who refused to send out gay information, Ann became a telephone counsellor for Dundee Lesbian, Bisexual & Gay Switchboard, where she is able to advise about sexual problems and help others to understand the issues involved in being both lesbian and disabled.

Trying to find relevant accessible information or make contact with other disabled lesbians is very hit-and-miss, so much depending upon sheer luck or circumstance. Over the years there has been much discussion about developing an information and befriending service specifically for disabled lesbians, bisexuals and gay men, offering accurate, accessible information on venues, services and counselling by disabled lesbians and gays. To date this has not happened, largely owing to the 'apparent' complexities of belonging to two communities, yet not fitting into either. Many funding bodies appear 'nervous' of supporting lesbian and gay initiatives, even if these initiatives could save lives. However, REGARD, the National Campaigning Organisation of Disabled Lesbians and Gay Men, will continue to pursue the matter, as part of its strategy to end the damaging isolation reported by so many members.

Abuse/sexual abuse

Sadly, like their heterosexual sisters, disabled lesbians and bisexual women are also victims of abuse. Most women were abused as children but some women are currently in abusive situations compounded by their economic or physical dependence on care-givers. This subject has been addressed in a separate chapter in order to give the matter the attention it deserves (see page 106). However, it is important to state here that at interview lesbians felt strongly that they were homosexual out of choice and not as a result of abuse.

Lesbian mothers

Most disabled women in our study stated that they were not expected to become wives or mothers. For disabled lesbians there are additional problems of negative stigma and prejudice, apart from the soul-searching and practical arrangements that require tact, diplomacy and an enormous effort to avoid potentially disastrous situations. Sadly, lesbians are still generally perceived as 'deviant' and considered 'ball-breakers' and 'man-haters' rather than women who prefer and love women. As 'unnatural' women, lesbians are not considered fit to be mothers, and all too often obstacles are placed in their way, so ensuring that motherhood has to be fought for.

Even in the 'enlightened' 1990s, when it has almost become chic to be lesbian, there are lesbians (disabled and non-disabled) in stable relationships, with homes and economic security, who are refused the opportunity to adopt children. As one lesbian pointed out,

> They would sooner keep children in homes where there are 20 children to one care worker ... than let us adopt a child and give it a good home and upbringing.

The fact that women are in stable relationships or in well-paid professional jobs does not count for much. The issue is not whether we are maternal, capable, employed or non-disabled, it is about the fact that women who love women within a homophobic society must pay a price. Having an impairment in addition to one's 'sexual deviance' means the odds are stacked way too high against most disabled lesbians becoming mothers. Jill explains,

> I went through a full assessment in order to adopt a child, but was rejected by the panel because I was a lesbian. They were concerned about my impairment but that wasn't the issue.

As Judy told us,

> I had my children within a marriage before I came out as a lesbian. It's when they go to school that it can become difficult as their difference is confirmed. Other children can be cruel. However, they cope and are great kids. I don't know if I would have had the courage to have children after I had come out; I guess it depends on the kind of support you have and whether you're in a stable relationship, etc.

All too often, because we have low self-esteem and we are told we are unfit mothers because of our disability or because we are lesbian, we cave in under the pressure and accept the judgement of others. As Gloria states,

> I left after one little argument and I couldn't go back … I didn't see myself as a good enough mother anyway, so I left them behind. He could do a better job than me. I now realise I was a bloody good mother but it's all too late now. The courts have made a ruling. I have liberal access but he won't allow me to live in the house again. I would love to live with them again. For years he told me what a bad mother I was, a useless housewife … and I believed it. It's a bit like my family, you can't do this or that. He just carried on where they left off.

Some lesbians choose artificial insemination by donor (AID) to conceive children. This requires a great deal of thought and planning and almost always presents lesbians with dilemmas about choice of and role, if any, of the donor. For those women who attend clinics where frozen semen is used and donors are anonymous, there are different issues. The point to emphasise is that this process is considered and the pros and cons measured. Naoise explains the complexities of deciding to have a child by self-insemination:

> As a lesbian who had a breakdown, I was very aware of requiring a network of support, while also being aware that being a parent is the bottom line in that it's something you can't delegate when things get tough but that you can accept and organise help. As a result of my breakdown I am a much more flexible and relaxed parent with different 'values' from before my breakdown and I'm more comfortable with good enough parenting. I don't have to be perfect, neither do my sons. The issue with AID is that you have to sit down and think about it; you have to commit yourself to it in the context of a world that is hostile to lesbians and to mental health system survivors.

Lesbians have, and probably always will have, children. We wrongly tend to think of AID as something new, something this generation of women has only recently discovered. Lesbians, like most heterosexual women, sometimes feel broody and have ideas about mothering. They have obvious obstacles to overcome, but do so ingeniously. It seems that whether lesbian, bisexual or heterosexual women, motherhood is something that they contemplate and accept or reject. If a lesbian decides motherhood is for her, she will usually find the means. As Naoise explains,

> The most difficult part was organising the donor's sperm at the time when I was most fertile. Clinics were out, because we wanted to conceive our child in our bed and we did so first time around.

However, most lesbians are aware of the opposition to their mothering and of the prejudice they may encounter. As Anna explains,

> We have discussed issues of parenting as my partner would like to have a child. We are aware of the attitude towards parents who are disabled or lesbian, but think what's important is that we carefully consider the implications and then decide.

Kay explains,

> We have three children, two from a former relationship and one by [artificial] insemination. The way they came into the world may be important to them at some stage, but more important is that they are wanted, planned for and loved. Providing the environment for them to grow into healthy, sensitive, loving adults is our goal. If we succeed, they will be able to cope with the whys and wherefores of their birth.

It's our community too

The 'body beautiful' and youth culture of present-day Western society can be a tyranny for very many women, disabled and non-disabled. However, many disabled lesbians and bisexual women have experienced alienation rather than nurturing and support from the lesbian and gay community.

Jenny described her disappointment at discovering that her community was as discriminatory as the rest of the world:

> When I decided to live as a lesbian, I thought it would be easier, because we all, lesbians and gay men, suffer oppression, therefore they won't oppress me. I quickly found that the same prejudice that we experience in the non-lesbian and

gay community was just as prevalent, and why shouldn't it be? I was incredibly disappointed because I expected lesbians and gay men to be more 'understanding', more 'sympathetic', more 'aware'. It is also true to say that some are more aware and realise that currently the community is not acceptable and have the intention and the will to do something about it.

Unfortunately, the lesbian and gay community may find it harder to integrate its disabled members now that they live with the experience or knowledge of AIDS. Undoubtedly, AIDS has had a negative impact on the gay community and generated a great deal of fear and resentment. Some lesbians and gay men out for the evening in a gay club just want to have fun and not be reminded of loved ones who are HIV-positive or have died with AIDS. They feel powerless to change things and resent having disabled people around to remind them of 'illness'. Conversely, there are lesbians and gay men who, because of their experience of HIV/AIDS, are more receptive to the needs of disabled lesbians and gay men and more accommodating to them.

Some women express a preference for lesbian-only space; they feel safer and believe that gay men can be as oppressive as any other men. After all, the lesbian and gay community is a diverse one, with many differences of politics, beliefs and expressions of sexuality. Elizabeth says,

Lesbians are better apart. Gay men dominate lesbians too much, just as in the heterosexual world.

Sara explains how she felt different on the gay scene after becoming disabled:

I felt I didn't belong fully to the lesbian scene any more, but neither did I fit in with disabled heterosexuals. I felt very alone and isolated for the first time in my life. I find lesbians are too posy and wanting to be 'beautiful' and I don't fit in. Some of my friends make an effort to go to accessible places sometimes but find them boring because everyone is somewhere else that we know I can't get into easily. Sometimes I get so lonely; I go to an inaccessible place and get carried in and take my own toilet in my van. However, this takes a lot of energy and is not always practical.

Dorothy says,

I no longer go on the lesbian and gay scene, I got pissed off with it. My partner and I and our friends now socialise in each other's homes.

Discomfort or discrimination in the disability community?

Unlike their heterosexual sisters, disabled lesbians and bisexual women were cautious about their place in the disability community. If sexuality is discussed at all, it is heterosexuality which is apparently the only acceptable form of sexual identity. Disabled lesbians had on many occasions tried to explain that issues such as Independent Living and personal assistance, or even transport, had different aspects to be considered for lesbians. However, disabled lesbians were often silenced or ignored. REGARD, the organisation of disabled lesbians and gay men, was founded in 1989, specifically to address homophobia and ignorance within the disability community. Although much has been achieved and REGARD was successful in placing equal opportunities firmly on the agenda of the British Council of Disabled People (the umbrella organisation of the disabled people's movement), there is still a lack of awareness, especially among heterosexual disabled men, resulting in offensive comments and oppressive practices. As Dorothy explains,

> *I'm out as a lesbian everywhere, but have to put up with the left-wing macho b*******, who have got such a lot to learn. I just have a go* [in response to their sexism and homophobia] *and have to battle on.*

Lesbians have experienced considerable homophobia in the disability community. We have been avoided, shunned and told that our lifestyles and loves are not as valid as heterosexual ones. We have even been subjected to verbal abuse, as Julie describes:

> *On a 'Rights Not Charity' demonstration, a group of deaf disabled marchers refused to march alongside those of us carrying the Lesbians & Gays with Disabilities banner. They said they didn't want to be associated with perverts!*

Thus, disabled lesbians and bisexual women can feel they do not belong to any community. They have to struggle to be part of communities which are oppressive and excluding.

Places to meet

When disabled women were asked where they met their partners, 43.09 per cent said in clubs, 40.33 per cent said 'in pubs' and 46.96 per cent said 'at work'. However, the largest group of women – 70.72 per cent (see Appendix 3, Fig. 41) – stated that they met their partners in other places, including meetings, conferences, seminars and rallies and one contributor stated she met her last lover at a funeral. Thus, it would appear that although work offers obvious economic and social benefits, including the money to pay to go to clubs and pubs, it seems that without those advantages, disabled women make the best opportunity of what is available to them.

As stated earlier, some women do not feel it is safe to be openly lesbian or bisexual and this can add to their isolation. Dorothy lives in what she describes as a 'frozen waste-land', in an ex-mining community, miles from anywhere. She says,

> *There is nothing here for lesbians. I look like a very big butch woman, and the locals give me a wide berth.*

She has contacted the nearest lesbian line but the volunteers are usually young, immature women who have not got a clue about life as a disabled lesbian. Although she is in a long-term relationship and her partner is 'brilliant', she would appreciate another disabled lesbian to talk to.

Born or acquired disability

The women interviewed all expressed a difference between their perceptions of women who were born disabled and of those who acquired a disability later in life. Some congenitally disabled women felt that they were more disadvantaged by special education, segregation and institutionalisation, resulting in social isolation or lack of opportunity to develop social skills. Others felt they were at an advantage, in that they did not have to make the transition from non-disabled to disabled, with resultant loss of social status, sudden unemployment and broken relationships resulting from that change. Ann explains,

> *I walked out of my home and I returned ten months later, paralysed and a completely different person. I had to accept my disability and get on with it. I always knew I was a lesbian as I had crushes on girls at school, even nurses in the hospital, but coping with disability was more pressing. My sexuality had to be put on hold while I sorted out the practicalities of living with a disability.*

While women who acquired a disability recognised that they were at an advantage by having lived as non-disabled people, they felt they were not taken seriously in the disability community. Brenda states,

I have a lot of confidence which some congenitally disabled people lack. However, there is a hierarchy of oppression in the disability movement and we are not taken seriously.

They felt there was a 'pecking order' and they were at the back of the queue.

Some women who acquired a disability later in life felt that there was nothing to be gained in identifying with a devalued group. This overwhelming negativity in the representation of disabled women made the transition from a non-disabled to a disabled identity even more difficult. It would appear that some women prefer to pass as non-disabled or remain 'ill', rather than adopt a potentially derogatory label. Some congenitally disabled women whose impairments were not obvious or who did not view themselves as disabled also struggled with the concept of identification as disabled. Gloria explains how after leaving special school she 'left her disability behind' for 20 years:

Disability is such an horrendous thing to carry around with you. It's a weight especially if you can get by – my impairment was slight. I never told my children. When I had to tell someone, it was like confession time, I felt as if I had a terrible disease.

Bridie explains the initial impact of disability on her life:

While going through the bereavement stage of acquiring a disability, I felt 'less of a person'. The search for a 'cure' meant that I did not feel sexy. Chronic pain meant that I felt tearful and out of control a high percentage of the time.

While there are obvious differences in each individual situation, those lesbians or bisexual women in our study who acquired a disability later in life were generally more confident and had more experience of sexual relationships. They were more prepared to enter into these relationships and negotiate for what they wanted, should the 'right' woman come along.

Conclusion

Although disabled women as a whole do not appear to talk to each other about sex, lesbians seem more prepared than heterosexuals to enter into open, honest dialogue about sexual matters. This difference was born out at a SHE seminar which had a 100 per cent attendance rate by those disabled lesbians who were invited. The seminar provided an opportunity for disabled lesbians to comment on the project to date and to talk openly in the group about their hopes and wishes for the future. It could be argued that lesbians are familiar with discussing sex because they are commonly confronted about their lesbianism. They have to deal with abusive comments from strangers on the street and are frequently presented with negative stereotypes in the media. Many lesbians are continually 'negotiating' their sexuality with family and colleagues. It may be this necessity to address their sexuality that makes discussion about sex possible, while their heterosexual sisters struggle to find a voice.

Although disabled lesbians and bisexual women have been adequately represented in this study, as a proportion of the total, most were white (including Irish women), with an average age of 30. The fact that black and younger disabled lesbians and lesbians with learning difficulties were not well represented says much about the level of safety in terms of perceived confidentiality required in order to enable these women to come forward.

Discussion with REGARD revealed a reluctance on behalf of black disabled lesbians to 'come out' and be identified. The reason put forward was homophobia in the disability community. Black disabled lesbians did not feel the disability community was a safe place to be out. There were also problems of anti-lesbianism within families and minority ethnic communities in addition there was lack of support to tackle the hostility that asserting their sexuality aroused.

We know from the study that 58.01 per cent of disabled women want further opportunities to discuss sex in a safe place (see Appendix 3, Fig. 49). Further work needs to be done to gain the trust of disabled women and develop understanding within all communities, to ensure that all disabled women's views are fully represented in future research.

The sexual health & equality hypotheses – Testing the hypotheses
for disabled lesbians and bisexual women

1. That there is inadequate sex education for disabled women, particularly those born disabled

Of the women in the study who were born disabled, 38.70 per cent received no sex education compared to 44.44 per cent of women who acquired their disability later in life (see Appendix 3, Fig. 19). The hypothesis is upheld for lesbians, as sex education is usually taught in the early to mid-teens prior to the development or declaration of sexual identity. Therefore the statistics for disabled heterosexual women apply to lesbians and bisexual women and the hypothesis is upheld.

2. That disabled women who acquired a disability later in life are more likely than those born disabled to be in a sexual relationship or have had sexual partners

Of the women who became disabled later in life and between the ages of 21 and 50, 56 per cent were in a sexual relationship (see Appendix 3, Fig. 18). Of the women who became disabled at between 31 and 35 years of age, 66.66 per cent were in a relationship. The hypothesis is borne out for lesbians and bisexual women, in that the women who were confident about their sexual identity were able to continue forming sexual relationships after impairment.

3. That race and/or religion influence sexual choices, e.g. lesbianism

Of all the disabled women in the study, 31.74 per cent (see Appendix 3, Fig. 17) stated that religion influenced their sexual choices and 60 per cent stated that their ethnic origin influenced their sexual choices (see Appendix 3, Fig. 32). This was upheld for the lesbians and bisexual women who are reflected in these statistics and provided additional relevant evidence at interview to support the hypothesis.

4. That there is a lack of relevant information about sex

Of all the disabled women in the study, 46.96 per cent (see Appendix 3, Fig. 16) stated they wanted more information about sex. This was upheld for lesbians (52 per cent) and, to a lesser degree, for bisexual women (25 per cent) who want more relevant, accessible information about sexuality and sexual practice. At interview 100 per cent of lesbians wanted accessible and appropriate information about lesbian sex, relevant to them as disabled lesbians.

5. That disabled women lack positive role models to improve self-esteem

The hypothesis is upheld for disabled lesbians and bisexual women who also lack positive role models. 52 per cent of lesbians, 55 per cent of bisexual women and 54.81 per cent of heterosexual women stated that they had no positive role models (see Appendix 3, Fig. 15).

6. That disabled women experienced sexual and other forms of abuse

Of the women in the study, 41.99 per cent experienced sexual abuse (see Appendix 3, Fig.9), 48.07 per cent had experienced other forms of abuse (see Appendix 3, Figs. 11 and 12) and 30.30 per cent of all women stated that disability contributed to the abuse (see Appendix 3, Fig. 13). The hypothesis is upheld for disabled lesbians and bisexual women. At interview it was revealed that most of the sexual abuse occurred during childhood, therefore sexual identity is not so relevant. However, disabled lesbians are subject to other forms of abuse as a result of their sexual identity and gave evidence at interview that abuse had directly or indirectly caused their impairment.

7. That disabled women do not practise safer sex

The statistics demonstrate that only 34.80 per cent of heterosexual women practise safer sex, as opposed to 35 per cent of bisexual women and 40 per cent of lesbians. This is a relatively low figure for the level of knowledge about HIV transmission demonstrated at interview by disabled lesbians. However a 'No, I don't practise safer sex' could be interpreted as 'I do not engage in sexual practices that involve risk'. The hypothesis was not upheld for lesbians.

8. That disabled women are reluctant to talk to each other about sex, but will talk to other people about it

Of the disabled lesbians in the study, 64 per cent talked about sex to other disabled women (see Appendix 3, Fig. 24 (i)) and 84 per cent talked to non-disabled women about sex (see Appendix 3, Fig. 24 (ii)). Although the statistics show a preference towards non-disabled women, the seminar held by the researchers for disabled women illustrated disabled lesbians' preparedness to discuss issues openly. The hypothesis was not upheld for lesbians.

1991 TIME-BOMB

I shall call you
(for the purposes of this piece
as they say),
Fiona.

And you would,
if you had the guts to recognise yourselves,
doubtless feel outraged
at sharing this collective name.

Dear Fiona,

you treat me
like a time-bomb
ever since I told you
that last summer
I went mad.

I count myself unfortunate –
friendships don't come easy to me.
So each time, Fiona,
you have withdrawn
or laughed in that frenzied way
or backed out of seeing me ...

You each display
only slightly different symptoms of
'I don't want to be anywhere near this nutter'.

You are all so busy
running away, Fiona
that even if I listed out your names,
and addresses,
none of you
would recognise
your right-on selves here, Fiona.

But even so
I had believed us
that treasured gem … friends.
So each time, Fiona,
you display
your narrow range of symptoms
it has hurt with the dull pain
of an old injury.

Dear Fiona,
you treat me
like a time-bomb
ever since I told you
that last summer
I went mad.
Unless you stop,
one of these days,
I may well
go off.

Char March

Chapter 3

Loving men

Issues for heterosexual disabled women

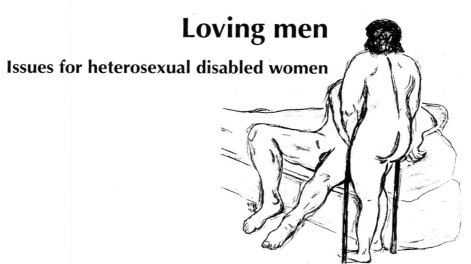

This chapter is based on the responses of the 135 heterosexual women who returned the SHE questionnaire, on interviews with 20 heterosexual women and on submitted written accounts about experiences of the development of their sexuality.

The areas covered in this part of the SHE research on sexuality overlap with those of the other two groups. Some issues kept recurring for heterosexual women, such as marriage, mothering and contraception. Relationships, parental views and societal views are also recurring themes. The women interviewed also explored other issues to do with the development of their sexuality and the recurring theme was inadequate sex education from teachers or parents. It took time to build a rapport with some of the women before they felt safe enough to be interviewed. However, once they agreed they would talk avidly, often without pausing for breath. It was as if these issues had been bursting to get out for years.

Knowledge denied

One woman, who grew up in institutional care, left school without really knowing how women became pregnant. How the lack of very basic sex education had had a negative impact on disabled women's ability to form relationships was highlighted by all women who were interviewed. It is evident that the basic right to knowledge is often denied disabled women when it covers that little three-letter word, SEX.

In a society that denies disabled people their rights, it is no surprise to learn that disabled women have reported receiving virtually no information about sex either when they were growing up or later on as adults. 42.54 per cent of disabled women in the study received no sex education (see Appendix 3, Fig. 19). The education system failed them by denying them sex education, even though this forms part of the National Curriculum. Their experiences highlight the lack of support many disabled women experience throughout their formative years and even into adulthood.

Sukie went to a special school. She said,

We were never taught about sex at school, it was as if it never existed. My parents never talked about it to me either.

Her earliest memories are that she was not seen as a sexual person by anyone around her. She grew up feeling that her disability was somehow responsible for this asexual response. She recalls,

> I soon learnt not to stand too close to my mother if she stopped to talk to a friend in the street because if I came into the conversation she would turn and lift up my skirt to show how my legs bent. There was no consideration as to how I would feel about my clothes being pulled up and my body being exposed to just anybody.

Apart from growing up feeling that disability is the cause of the 'asexual' labels that are thrust on them, some disabled women are also left completely unprepared for the physical changes that puberty brings on. During Sukie's adolescence she was given no preparation for menstruation. The first thing she knew about this was when her mother turned up at school and said,

> Oh dear, you have been taken queer. You had better go and see the nurse.

The nurse then explained to her that she had had her period.

This kind of rude awakening in learning to understand their bodies is not unusual for disabled girls to experience. It is as if this important change from girlhood to womanhood is not going to happen for them and when, of course, it does, this is hurriedly explained without any thought given to the developing woman inside.

When Sukie went to training college she experienced sex for the first time. She was 16 years old and over the years she had learnt from school chums and her own reading what sex was all about. She went to the family planning clinic to get contraceptive advice before starting college. She managed to get the Pill and was feeling pleased with herself for having taken precautions and been 'sensible'. She told her mother, looking for some encouragement,

> I thought I would let her know that I was going to protect myself and hoped that she would be pleased that I was acting in a responsible and mature way.

But her mother's response was to say, 'Don't talk to me about that.' Sukie said,

> That was the first and last time I ever talked to my mum about sex.

The lack of sex information can leave women ill-equipped to form sexual relationships. Sukie added,

> *In those days sex to me was just the sex act and it was sex for sex sake; there were no relationships going along with it.*

While she was at training college she became quite promiscuous and it was as if all the sex education that had been withheld from her owing to her disability exploded inside her, finding release just in sexual encounters without any emotional satisfaction, just physical sex. Sukie said,

> *In some ways it was a fun time but in other ways it wasn't. I am just glad it was pre-AIDS time: I really had lots of partners.*

She could not separate the sexual act from love and thought, 'Oh good, someone wants sex with me so they must love me'. She mistook sex for love.

DIY learning

When children are not given correct information about sexuality, they will try to find out for themselves. This is not adequate for any child because there is the potential to get the facts wrong, possibly leading to an unplanned pregnancy or the risk of contracting sexually transmitted diseases, including HIV.

Lack of information on sexual matters and having to find out the facts of life for oneself was what happened to eleven of the women that were interviewed. Ruby said,

> *I still remember fondly one summer holiday when my best friend told me all about sex and I felt good that I knew all there was to know on that subject.*

However, one of her teachers seemed to indicate that she felt Ruby could be at risk from pregnancy and took it upon herself to draw her aside and warn her. Ruby felt that her flirty nature had been the reason for this warning. She remembers that someone came in from outside to do a short session about birth control, and that was the extent of Ruby's formal sex education.

Tina, too, remembers scant sex education, and most of what she knew at the time was from her biology class and from older children:

When I was in the fifth form the family planning nurse came in and did two sessions. One was on birth control and the other was on sexually transmitted diseases. We were taught that some men who developed venereal diseases that were left untreated would develop sexually perverted tendencies or fetishes and then might target in on disabled women because that was 'different'.

This kind of misinformation had an impact on Tina a little later on when she was being pursued by a man:

I didn't know how to react to him and I can remember thinking, 'What if he has got VD?' I was young then and believed what I had been told.

Information that is acquired in secret can result in guilt, as Crystal remembers. One of her school friends had got hold of her parents' sex books and would avidly copy out extracts to take to school each day. Bits of scribbled information were passed around and what they did not know for fact was made up. Crystal recalls with sadness that her friend's parents became suspicious about their daughter reading their sex book, and it was put out of her reach:

I felt guilty about getting my knowledge in this way. We knew that it was underhand but we were devastated when she could no longer get bits of information on sex from her parents' book.

However, by the time that happened they at least had a basic working knowledge.

Sex was taboo at home for Crystal:

If anything came on the television that was considered too sexy, it was quickly turned off. Once my periods started my mother told me not to allow boys to touch me 'down there' as it was dangerous. I cannot remember any other conversations about sex at home during my childhood.

The other women interviewed had similar tales to tell. Pandora said,

When I was 18 I did not know how you got pregnant and I thought this could happen just by heavy petting. I kept myself to myself for years because I felt such low self-esteem.

While we live in a society where communication on sex does not necessarily flow between parents and children, at least most able-bodied children will learn the basic facts at school. The above examples show how some disabled women are left in total ignorance, not just from over-protective parents but also by the education system. This kind of ignorance can leave disabled children vulnerable, confused, open to abuse and feeling guilty. Knowledge, after all, is power and gives people confidence.

Lack of positive role models

Lack of information starts to create a web of disempowerment that is not just restricted to how we feel about ourselves but also has repercussions on how other people see us. In the survey 54.14 per cent of disabled women said that they did not have positive role models (see Appendix 3, Fig. 29). Sukie talked about how this had affected her in the past and how she was looking forward to the day when much more information is available, including resource books on mothering and on sexual positions for disabled women. Her experiences demonstrate how we are seen and treated by others as if our relationships were inferior:

> I have never been made to feel that I am a sexual being either at school or by my parents. I feel sexy inside, though, and my husband sees me as such but not other people.

She says that because her husband is able-bodied he is not looked on as her 'husband' but rather her carer. On one of her few requests to social services she asked for a bath aid to help her get into the bath. The social worker had said that she did not need anything as her husband could help her in and out. Sukie's response was,

> In that case, if I have an argument with my husband and I am not talking to him, does that mean I will not get a bath?

She feels that her relationship is looked on by others either in a critical way as in 'Why is he with a disabled woman?' or 'Oh dear, he must have to do a lot of work in looking after her'.

This research has shown that 40.88 per cent of disabled heterosexual women said they did not have positive disabled role models and that this has had a major impact on their lives, from earliest experiences to coping with being a disabled mother. Early memories that Ruby encountered followed that of other children of her age group with crushes on pop stars. All children go through this stage, but when disability becomes more apparent this development starts to make changes in what we expect for ourselves as sexual awareness develops. Ruby said,

> I can remember being in love with Paul McCartney of the Beatles and this lasted for a number of years. Later I fell in love with a classmate. I can vividly remember when my hormones raced. I was eleven and he was 16 and this was my very first relationship.

This did not include sex but involved spending time together by going around to his house, playing records and feeling 'in love'. These platonic relationships appeared to be the norm at the day-school for physically disabled children she was then attending. She remembers that one of the senior girls was already engaged and she was surprised at this. To her eleven years the couple seemed very mature. This role model had impressed her as the young woman was substantially disabled and her fiancé was able-bodied.

Crystal's earliest experiences started in the same way as Ruby's. At school she had the usual school-girl crushes on the boys there but although she continued to fall in and out of love often, she did not have a particular romantic relationship during her school years:

> All the boys seemed to be chasing the more able girls and did not seem to see the ones that were more severely disabled.

Ruby was already starting to look for role models for her identity as she went from crushes and platonic relationships to seeing into her own possible future. She had noted that disabled women did form relationships that had potential in securing partners and had also noted with surprise that disability could break out of restricting roles. However, even at eleven she was already beginning to take note that this was not going to be an easy path to follow. Crystal was also coming to the same conclusion:

> I was beginning to feel the pressures there are on us to be as able-bodied as possible.

Ruby remembers when two possible relationships failed to develop. Although she had wanted these two friendships to develop, they didn't and she felt that disability and concepts of beauty were the issues in these two instances:

If I had been stunningly beautiful and disabled maybe things would have been different.

Would Ruby have felt that 'stunning beauty' would have made a difference for her if she had had strong positive disabled role models? As positive role models do not depend necessarily on how people look, the answer to this would be 'No'. Owing to the lack of positive disabled role models, there is the temptation to look at ourselves as wanting in some way rather than focusing on the restrictions placed upon us to create emotional isolation. Ruby herself realised that another reason for being emotionally isolated was the lack of opportunity to meet people. Unlike Ruby, there are still many disabled women who do not see society's barriers but rather see themselves as the problem.

Positive role models would go towards helping to build the kind of services that disabled women need. Sukie has felt the negative side of this lack of role models in relation to services. As her babies grew up she became increasingly frustrated about inaccessible crèche facilities. This gave messages to her that society does not expect disabled women to have babies. She remembers how, just five years ago at a disability organisation's AGM, no crèche was provided, which just reinforced her oppression. She feels that disabled women will have started to make their point when disabled mothers appear on baby adverts:

At one time there were just white babies on adverts but although that has changed now there are still no disabled mothers or disabled babies on them.

Sukie still feels that this lack of positive images is affecting her life today. She feels the signs are many that say disabled people do not have sexual relationships or children. For instance, she recently went on holiday to Scotland to a place which advertised accommodation suitable for disabled people. When they got there, they found there were no double beds at all and the bath was not accessible. She felt that they should have advertised it as holidays for disabled people and their carers only! They had booked for three weeks and had to sleep apart. As they were leaving, they saw another family booking in where the mother was disabled and they wondered what they would feel like when they saw the bedrooms. Sukie said,

I was too embarrassed to bring up the issue at the time but I intend to write to them now that I am back.

She said that she constantly lives in a culture that denies her existence and finds that television is the worst arena for perpetuating this isolating image. She said,

> *The only time sex and disability comes up is on the disability programmes. The rest of the mainstream programmes hardly mention it at all.*

Positive role models for disabled women, either from the disability movement or from the media are hard to find. Without them disabled women are restricted in how they formulate a clear identity. To start to rectify this situation, concerted work needs to be done among disabled women, with service agencies and through the media network.

Sexual abuse

The incidence of sexual abuse was high throughout this survey, with 41.99 per cent of the disabled women interviewed having experienced it (see Appendix 3, Fig. 8). Crystal's experience shows how easily abuse can start to take place and illustrates how vulnerable disabled women are, through their own lack of strength, to over-protective parents and because help is needed to get away from dangerous situations. The study shows that not being 'streetwise', being educated at sheltered schools and poor judgement through lack of information all contribute to disabled women being vulnerable to abuse.

Crystal had parents who were over-protective. She had one girlfriend who lived nearby and although she was disabled, she could walk and push Crystal in her chair. They would spend hours in a local café, eyeing up young men. The men who ran this café were much older than they. As Crystal and her friend hung around often, it was not long before the men invited them to their flat upstairs.

Crystal was carried up a fire escape at the back and once inside was nearly raped. She was terrified that she might be pregnant, although full sexual penetration had not actually taken place. Crystal recalls,

> *I just did not know how near sperm had to come to me before I could become pregnant and I was 16 years old!*

Crystal had an agonising month waiting to see whether she was pregnant and had no one to whom to relate this experience.

It would have been impossible for Crystal to get out on her own. She was totally vulnerable, having had to be carried up the stairs in the first place. Crystal was lucky but her experience shows how disability makes women vulnerable. Coupled with her lack of sexual knowledge, she had an awful experience which could have turned out worse. Many other disabled women are not so lucky as Crystal. Their dependence on others for help or care leaves them in a position of isolation and at risk.

Low self-esteem about being disabled and unloved can mean that disabled women tolerate abuse to get affection. Pandora said,

> *I felt that because I was disabled, men would not want to look at me. There are plenty of able-bodied women out there. When a married man started to take me out, I put up with a lot of sexual abuse. He only wanted me for sex. That was very painful. Although today I don't feel I am damaged, I was at the time. I am now in my sixties and when this happened, I was very young. I just wish I had had someone to talk to. It was so painful.*

Today, few disabled people achieve full-time employment and fear of losing a job can result in having to tolerate abuse at work, which was Ellen's experience. Her boss would come up and ask if the splinters in the desk were a bother. She said,

> *He would come up behind me and use the splinter excuse to touch me under the table or brush his hands against my breast. There was not much I could do about it and I did not feel that I could tell anybody.*

Isolation

All of the women interviewed said they had experienced isolation. This has appeared within families, special schools, boarding schools and institutional care. The women with hidden disabilities also experienced isolation through fear of their disabilities becoming known. From these accounts a picture emerges of how harmful segregation is to every avenue of our lives. Isolation crops up as emotional and physical restrictions, each having an impact on our quality of life and happiness. It erodes every corner of our existence, creating disempowerment in its wake. When it dissolves for a period of time, its reoccurrence is still a shock. Of the women I interviewed, 40 per cent said that home life itself can be the most disempowering environment to live in as disabled girls or young women. An ability to make friends in childhood forms the basis for our adult relationships, yet these early encounters can be thwarted, bringing isolation at an early age.

Sukie's isolation became more acute when she was forced to change schools. Initially she went to her local school which was run by nuns but when she had to go into a class that was upstairs, the nuns said that she should start to go to a special school. They would not accept that Sukie could negotiate the steps even though she had to at home. They said they were concerned that other children might knock her over and virtually told her mother that she had to be withdrawn. She was then sent to a special school that involved a coach journey as it was several miles from where she lived:

> When I went to this special school, of course I could not see my new friends in the evenings as they did not live near me.

She was seven when she had to leave her first school and all her local friends.

It was many years later that Sukie experienced freedom at college and loved every minute of it. When she went back home she found it hard, once more, to form relationships. She did not go out much and had few friends, so the opportunities for her as a disabled woman to make relationships were again few. Our society does not encourage the participation of disabled people the community's social life, and Sukie felt this strongly in her sudden renewed isolation after training college.

Ruby found sharp contrast between her experiences at day-school and her subsequent experiences at boarding school. The boarding school was single-sex and situated in an isolated part of the country so from the age of 14 she had no experiences of relationships with boys at all. She had had expectations of relationships continuing because at her day-school she was very popular, and the school was in a city. Once out in the country things changed for her drastically. This was quite a let-down for her, as she wanted to continue meeting boys:

> I have often pondered long and hard on whether that segregation has had an effect on me today.

When Ruby left school the wilderness in the field of relationships continued and she began to feel quite depressed. Once back at home she, like other women interviewed, had few opportunities for meeting people. She found that the ages of between 18 to 21 were bleak and she did not meet anybody to form a relationship with. She had started work but this did not relieve this situation:

I still wrestle with this notion. Are the things that happen to me to do with disability or are they to do with me? I am quite sure that disability has a part to play in this, but it is difficult to find out what the part is. I am loath to make sweeping statements, and access does play a part but I don't like pubs even if I can get in.

Despite having grown up in isolating educational institutions, Ruby, like other disabled women, still questions whether their circumstances are down to her rather than what has been happening to her. This is not unusual in a society that requires disabled people to be as able-bodied as possible rather than making changes that would ensure their participation.

The depression that results from isolation and rejection can threaten mental health. This was summed up by one of Tara's first comments during the interview:

I am finding this interview difficult now. I had wanted to talk about my feelings as a woman but as soon as I remember being rejected by my parents, I want to cry. The memories of rejection are painful, so we will keep this brief.

Tara does not have memories of an awakening sexuality and does not want a sexual relationship. She has been chaste by choice for more years than she can remember and wants her life to remain that way. She was born disabled and spent most of her life in a residential home. She left the institution some ten years ago and now lives in a flat that has supporting care attached. She said,

When you have lived in an institution for as long as I have, you start to like that kind of life. When I left I was excited but also missed the rigid hours that an institution sets. I used to sleep in a lot when I got my own place as I was not made to get up.

The biggest change to her sexuality is that she now feels free to have sexual relationships but chooses not to. Tara feels the biggest rejection was not from men, although they have rejected her, but her parents rejection by leaving her 'in care'. Her parents are both dead now but Tara has still not forgiven them.

Feeling sexy

Feeling sexy is important, and the women I interviewed had different views on this. In this survey, 63.54 per cent of disabled women said that they found it easy to express their sexuality (see Appendix 3, Fig. 61). However, Tara admits that institutional life did nothing to reinforce her feelings about being a woman. When a young girl grows up being seen as asexual throughout her childhood and most of her adult life, there is no opportunity to learn the basic interactions that are the foundation of forming sexual relationships or knowing how to relate to sexual partners. Confidence and self-esteem are not skills that grow within isolation. Without confidence or self-esteem, people cannot interact easily. We learn from our parents how to give and receive love. Tara's rejection by her parents would have left her at a disadvantage in the relationship stakes.

Dorothea has not been rejected and feels sexy most of the time. She says that sometimes she does not feel as sexy as she did when she was able-bodied:

> There are clothes I had when I was able-bodied that made me feel sexy but I don't feel the same wearing them now. That's because my mobility is different. I do feel sexy inside, though, and my boyfriend says I look sexy in all my clothes. We have a wonderful sex life. There isn't anything about sex that embarrasses me.

As disabled women get older, feeling sexy can be more of an effort. Ellen likes to take her sex life in the slow lane now and commented on sexuality and ageing:

> Doctors say that they understand about disability but I feel they just give it lip service. When I went through the change, I was not given any information at all. I think it is worse when you are disabled because so much information is lacking and this is a very lonely time. Disability becomes more difficult if we do not feel happy about our bodies. Younger disabled women have often told me that they are unhappy about how they feel in their bodies. I have felt unhappy about mine, too.

Heaven said that she feels sexy most of the time:

> The only thing that annoys me is I cannot move easily in bed. We just make up for limited movement in different ways. I don't see this as having a restricted sex life, just different. Anyway, I like to use my mouth quite a lot.

Jade also said that she feels sexy most of the time:

I know society does not see me as sexy and I am carrying a lot of weight but when I am with my lovers something else takes over. I have always had a large appetite for sex. I do wish that I could undress in a sexy way. I have to pull my clothes off using one arm so this does not look sexy. However, once they are off, I really start to enjoy myself. I cannot do a lot of different positions but it's still great.

Paula said that sex was better when she was younger:

I still feel sexy but there have been times when I would rather read a good book. Generally speaking my sex life is still good, just less frequent. I have had different partners, some able-bodied and some disabled. Always sex has been good. If you both have problems moving, think of something new to do. It's all loving at the end of the day.

Rejection

It is not just institutions that contribute towards isolation and ensuing depression, but also physical impairment which can and does result in rejection. Ruby feels at her most womanly when she has flirty moments and she has many of these, yet she feels that the personality she presents is because of her disability and that some men find her strange. Ruby feels that the worst state she can remember was when she had unrequited love. This has happened twice in her life to date and she equates these periods with feeling physically ill:

I can remember feeling intensely miserable, it was awful and I am sure I was rejected because of being disabled.

Although on these occasions she felt she was pursued because of her disability, the men in question did not want to actually have a sexual relationship with her. Ruby feels that there is a certain type of man who will lead disabled women on but really has no intention of having a full relationship with someone who is disabled:

Unfortunately at the time it is difficult to spot these types of men until it is too late.

Crystal became disabled in her first year of life and for her, awareness of her situation came as the first few years of her life unfolded. She recalls her sexuality blossoming before realising that she was disabled. Isolating awareness grew with her as her account explains. Crystal's earliest memories of her developing sexuality go back to the age of three. She recalls how she would fall in love at the drop of a hat with many boys from the age of four upwards. The feelings lasted for a few hours rather than days but she does remember the love and adoration that swept over her. Crystal was not aware of her disability until she was about five and was going to school. Although she had been disabled in her first year of life, she thought that she had just not learnt to walk yet and this would come with some sort of 'learning' that she had not experienced.

At around the age of three she remembers having spent some time in a children's home:

> My first taste of institution life was horrific. I remember eating institution food and feeling sick. Bed-wetting was punished and bullying by older children was the rule of the day.

She fell in love constantly for comfort as this somehow compensated her for being placed in care. She recalls hours of isolation as there were too few staff around to give individual attention and that she developed a habit of talking to herself, which she still has today. She was only there for two years but it seemed to her like a lifetime. Twice she tried to escape with one of her playmates pushing her on a go-cart, but they never got far out of the main gates before being spotted and were soon returned to the institution.

By the time she went to school, she began to realise that she was disabled and the school she went to was a so-called 'special' school. This was quite a few miles from where she lived, and this meant that her school friends did not live nearby. Crystal recalls,

> The end of the summer holidays was somehow the worst. On returning to school you always found that one or two of the children had died.

Her early school memories were filled with loss of school friends seemed to die each year. This was back in the mid-1950s and the death of friends was no stranger to her:

> It seemed to be par for the course when you went to a special school. Not all the children there had long life expectancy in those days. I suppose with antibiotics becoming more efficient this is not so today.

During her teens she was taken to Lourdes on a pilgrimage and fell in love with one of the helpers. He, however, only had eyes for the convent schoolgirls who were staying in the same hotel and, of course, were able-bodied. Like Ruby, Crystal has tales of unrequited love, only many more of them. She recalls that all the big loves in her life have been unrequited:

> I feel that this was largely due to my low self-esteem because of my disability. Somewhere in my mind it goes back to school days. The lack of expectation that I felt from teachers and family seems to have spilled over into my inability to form relationships. Of course the institution days have not helped either.

Crystal went to college and like other women that I interviewed, found sudden freedom and started to form sexual relationships. She decided that the best way for this to continue was to leave home and find a flat. This did not happen instantly. Initially, she left college to return home and once more came under the over-protectiveness of her parents. Crystal had a boyfriend when she left college and this continued for a while after she left. She said,

> They did not encourage this new love of my life to come around as they felt he was not suitable because of our age difference. We broke up and I was heart-broken.

Her able-bodied sisters and brothers could go out with anybody they liked but her relationships were heavily vetted by both parents. Crystal soon had no relationships at all and very few friends that lived nearby. She did manage to get her first job but it was a small firm and did not offer much contact with people of her own age. She drove an invalid carriage at that time and could go for drives, which broke up some of the humdrum existence that she experienced. In this instance, her parents' over-protectiveness put barriers up for her again. This left Crystal with the problem of trying to take them down on her own. She said,

> I had a girlfriend who lived in a ground-floor flat in London which I went to for weekends. This was fun but as she was also disabled we tended to stay in, experimenting with make-up or playing records.

Her father eventually put his foot down about these excursions as he was frightened that Crystal would get pregnant. The weekends were so innocent, with not a boyfriend in sight, but still she was stopped from going. She was 18 years old.

Some disabled women do not have the chance to get away from the restrictions of family life or institutions as accessible housing and supporting care are not always available. Independent living is still a relatively new concept, and resources to fund this are restricted by both central and local government. This section has highlighted some of the isolation that disabled women face but there are other forms of isolation that are not instantly apparent. Fear of disabilities becoming known can create a different kind of isolation. For example, three women I interviewed, who had hidden disabilities, all expressed fear and the need to keep a part of themselves secret.

Ginger, Sammy and Petra are close friends. They live in the same city and are all in their twenties. They became firm friends through a club which they belong to. All three say that life for them is different when they are going out with the club because only they know they are disabled. Petra said,

> *If people realised that I have had a disability, I know I would face prejudices in the same way that people face who have a seen disability. Able-bodied people are scared of differences and start to push away.*

Ginger and Sammy do have bouts of depression but can control them. Petra seldom experiences depression these days but would never tell a future employer about her past problems. All three say that it is not something they would ever highlight with their friends and, apart from relapses, they do not feel very disabled themselves. They feel that their sexuality is not affected by their disability but this is because their disabilities are not seen. Petra says that if prospective boyfriends found out, she would not be seen as desirable. Ginger and Sammy only partly agreed with this but also did not disclose their disabilities to partners until they were sure of the relationship being sound.

While there are no obvious restrictions on their image and sexuality, all three want to keep their disabilities a secret. They frequently experience fear about being found out as they are aware of the prejudices that they would start to face from employers and potential boyfriends. To have to hide a disability has its own isolating consequences and will rebound on confidence and levels of self-esteem. The fear of rejection does not go away and, like other disabled women I spoke to, they have to place a lot of trust in the people they become close to. If trust is ever misplaced they are as vulnerable as any other disabled women seeking to find partners in a society that segregates and penalises differences.

Sex talk

The survey has shown that 58.03 per cent of disabled women say that they talk to other disabled women about sex. Although this is just over half of the survey, of the 20 women I interviewed, only four said they did. There is a contradiction between respondents to the questionnaire and the women I interviewed. The interviewees commented that if we do not value ourselves, then it is likely that we will not value each other either.

Sukie talked about this during her interview. She said she sometimes feels that perhaps she is talking to the wrong group of disabled women but the disabled women she knows do not talk freely about sex:

> *I am not sure if this is connected with disabled women being reluctant to talk about their disability in general and therefore sex is not mentioned either, or if there are other reasons.*

Pandora and Tina also voiced this view. The women I interviewed felt more literature on sexuality would prove useful as well as having sexual literature that covered, for instance, sexual positions that can help with different disabilities. Pandora's comment on future sex discussion groups was supportive:

> *If my past experiences can help other women so that they don't have to go through the pain that I went through, I would be happy.*

Marriage

The expectation of marriage either by disabled women themselves or by their peers is, at its best, low and usually absent. In the survey, 29.28 per cent of disabled women said that as children they did not have expectations of getting married or having children (see Appendix 3, Fig. 7). In society as a whole, girls are expected to get married and have babies and if able-bodied children were asked the same question, they would probably all say 'Yes'. Disabled women do get married and divorced and live with their partners. Of the 20 women I interviewed, seven were married and of these, three had been divorced and one remarried. As the marriages progressed, each had different experiences of how her life had changed.

Sukie married the first man who asked her. Although she has no regrets about this having ended, for the first 18 months after her divorce she again experienced isolation and loneliness. She was busy trying to make ends meet but life was getting increasingly difficult as she tried to look after her two children. She was still working but had to take more time off when her children were sick. She would often pretend to her employer that it was she who was sick when it was really her children, so that it would not look as if she was having a lot of time off because of them. She joined Gingerbread (the association for one-parent families) and found some support, but there was no disability section of that organisation that she could join. If she were in that organisation today Sukie said she would raise the issue of disability much more than she did in the past.

Once the children were older, Sukie got them into a nursery and then she had freedom again during the day after she gave up work. The evenings were hard as she could not afford baby-sitters and she was lonely again. She started doing some voluntary work and met her second husband. The children went to their father's at the weekends, and this gave her some time to devote to her new relationship. Her second husband was able-bodied and she was worried how her new in-laws would accept her disability. It was hard but looking back over the last few years, she has managed to come through all the hurdles that appeared in her path. Now she feels that she is more challenging and has grown into a stronger person over the years.

Ruby got married when she was 21 years old. She said,

> The thing was that he was totally unsuitable. I was marooned at home with no one taking any interest in me at all, so I married him.

Ruby felt that she made compromises to get out of her domestic situation. She could see no other way to get out of living at home with her family. The marriage lasted just under two years before they broke up.

Sukie and Ruby went into their first marriages as a form of escape. However, if there had been more opportunities for them as disabled women, it is doubtful either would have gone down that path.

Ellen married her first lover and they have been together for 30 years now. She said,

> I did not go out with many men when I left school. I went to a school for able-bodied children but I was aware of my disability as I kept falling down. This left me feeling shy so I did not go out very much. I was once walked home from a social event and he kissed me. It was awful because he put his tongue into my

mouth. I did not see him again. In those days we were not encouraged to have lots of boyfriends anyway. I married my husband and he is the first and only man I have slept with.

Motherhood

Motherhood is another specific area which disabled women are reluctant to enter. In the survey, 44.75 per cent of disabled women said they were not expected to get pregnant (see Appendix 3, Fig. 57 (i)). One woman said she had developed a fear of her local social services department after her first child was born, as a result of their insensitive approach to her needs. Another fear disabled women experience is that society expects one not to cope and therefore people will judge one's mothering abilities against one's disability. Other women I interviewed either did not want babies at present or did not want them at all. Running out of time or changing their mind as they grew older were also reasons for not going into motherhood. There is also the pressure for perfection and disabled women come under this pressure quite heavily. Miranda is a disabled mother who had a disabled baby. She said,

The pressures are always there for women not to have anything but perfect babies.

Sukie was afraid of going to social services for help after her first child was born, in case they assumed that she could not cope and they would take the baby away from her. She felt she had to be as able-bodied as possible. Picking up the baby from the floor was difficult, and she would love to have had some sort of equipment to help her do this but was afraid to go for help. She eventually did get a social worker, who said that she would send Sukie and her baby on holiday. However, they ended up in a wing of a hospital under observation. Part of this wing had been made up as a flat in which they put Sukie to see how she would cope with the baby:

I was extremely angry and after three days I went off home. If it happened to me today, I would not stay as long as I did. Years later I saw my notes which made comments like 'got up late'. I had gone in good faith and thought I was on holiday so why should I get up early?

Sukie has rarely been near her social services department again. Although she felt it was total abuse of her civil liberties, she was too frightened to make a fuss at the time. Later she had another baby, but still she did not feel that she could ask social services for help, even though the going was tough. She recalls long periods of loneliness during this time because although she had a car, she could not get the carrycot into it. Once her husband had gone to work, she could not leave the house.

To date she feels that the contact she has had with social services has meant that her life is an open book. When she did go to social services about a cot, the officer with her file started talking about the time that her dog jumped up at the coach escort, which happened when she was about ten. She was now 21. This was another reason that she did not want to go for further help.

Sukie's experience with her social services' idea of support is more than enough to put any disabled woman off the thought of becoming a mother. It is now the time for disabled women to get to grips with all service delivery agencies and demand that they start delivering the types of services that empower and support them. Disabled mothers should certainly have control of how their services are delivered and as much support as they need.

Maria also had problems with the support agencies:

> *I noticed health visitors seemed to have such narrow views of disabled mothers. One started visiting every day and when I asked her why, she said that she was new and did not want to make a mistake. I complained and she was then changed.*

This health visitor was giving clear messages that she did not have confidence in Maria's mothering ability by visiting her every day.

Ruby never thought about having children at all. She has never wanted to adopt any either. She has seen women taken over by their children and finds this uncomfortable. Today she is 39 and is convinced that she is now too old to have any. When she was 21, she went to her consultant and told him she wanted to go on the Pill. The consultant said she should have babies instead, as lots of his patients had had them. Ruby was not the least interested in this suggestion but it is interesting to note that the medical profession can be helpful in supporting motherhood, although this is not always the case.

The situation for some disabled women is longing for rather than actually having babies. This was Crystal's experience. As a young girl she dreamt of having babies:

I always wanted four, two boys and two girls and yet I have never managed to find a relationship that would provide these for me.

When she lived with her first partner she felt that she was too young to have children:

I do not know where the time has gone and although I still dream of having children, I am now closer to 50 than I would like to be and know that this would now not be possible.

She knows that at her age adoption is also out of the question but still dreams on. Crystal was told by a consultant that children would be possible for her, and there was no reason why she could not have children. Her body-clock is now against her, and she seems resigned to the fact that now this will not happen unless she forms a relationship with a father.

If there had been more disabled mothers around, it is likely that Crystal would have found the time to have her own children:

I suppose fear played a part in my not having children, as well as running out of time.

Pandora also said that she wanted children but ran out of time:

When I was young I wanted children a lot. I longed for them, but now, looking back, I don't know whether I would have coped. It is such a responsibility. I don't know if my body would have coped. I am not sure I would have had the physical strength.

Crystal says that being disabled takes up most of her energy but with enough support she feels that her life would have been full of babies. Ginger, Sammy and Petra hope to have children eventually, although Petra wants to leave it as late as possible. They have fears for their future because they know that their disabilities could start to show more if their drugs go out of balance, but for now they are happy in their lives and babies can come later.

Rosebud's expectations of being a mother changed after her accident. She hated the new sexual role that she found herself in once she became disabled:

My parents had always expected me to get married and have children but now things are different.

Plans such as marriage and children were no longer discussed at home. Rosebud did eventually get married but not until many years later.

Ellen had one child and, like Sukie, found little support in being a disabled mother:

> *There was not much help around and no one to turn to. I just had to cope on my own. I had my husband to help and we had to just get on with it.*

Other disabled mothers that I spoke to also managed to cope. Gloria, Heaven, Sophie and Violet all said that they coped. This was either with the help of their partners or family. None of the women said that service delivery agencies had been very helpful.

The problems that disabled mothers and disabled women wanting to have babies face, need to be resolved by service delivery agencies becoming pro-active in their support and by their developing extra services specifically to support pregnant disabled women. Unless responsive services are developed, disabled mothers will continue to have a tough time throughout their pregnancy and early years of motherhood.

Relationships after disability

Some of the disabled women I interviewed talked about the compromises that they had had to make. For Rosebud this came in her teens, when she became disabled. Until then she had enjoyed an able-bodied existence and she recalls the drastic changes that were thrust upon her. Rosebud was 15 when she was involved in a car crash. She had gone to an ordinary school where she had many friends. Her earliest memories of her developing sexuality go back to when she was ten:

> *I can remember being interested in boys from a young age and I was convinced that I was in love at the age of ten. His name was Paul and he was in the same class.*

When she was 14, Rosebud had a relationship with a boy at the local college. They often went out together and their parents accepted that they had a relationship. This was largely platonic as Rosebud did not want to have sexual relations with anybody until she was married. This was not the norm among her school friends, but she had been brought up a Catholic and this was the path she was following.

After the car crash, she felt numb and angry. Her life changed so totally. Once she started to recover from the initial shock, her relationship crumbled. Her boyfriend said he would stay by her but as the months passed, he started going out with other women. She hardly remembers the pain of him passing as her life was so numb at the time.

Rosebud went back home to live with her parents after she was released from hospital. This proved difficult as her bedroom had been up a flight of steps and now she was in a much smaller room downstairs. Her friends helped her a lot in the beginning by giving support but as time went by they finished their exams and went to different colleges. Rose secured a place at a training college for disabled people to do a secretarial course. She had originally wanted to be a vet.

Rosebud said that the rejection she felt after becoming disabled stayed with her for a long time. She felt it from her boyfriend, family and friends. A couple of friends stayed in touch, but to this day she feels a distance between them:

> They changed their view of me and the things I could accomplish. It was lucky I did not change my view of myself or else I would have just given up.

Rosebud eventually managed to get into an accessible flat and for a while she got a job doing some secretarial work for a voluntary agency. She met her present husband seven years after her accident and has given up outside work to take up writing. Her husband runs his own business so she sometimes helps with his paperwork but mainly concentrates on her own writing of poetry. She said,

> I feel lucky in that I have achieved the things in life that I have always wanted despite becoming disabled yet I still have difficulty coping with the asexual view that society has of me.

She also feels the lack of opportunity to have had multiple relationships before settling down and often wonders if she will end up having an affair. Rosebud does not want children now but is not sure why. Her husband does not seem to want any either so in this respect they are happy.

Rosebud did not have full sexual relations before her accident and to this day she wonders how different this side of her relationship might have been if she had:

I love sex and I think I always will. If I had not been a Catholic my teen years would have been very different. I love my life now, my partner and my parents and friends but I can remember when I hated the world.

Rosebud has a clear view of herself as a young woman and a strong belief in her sexuality despite the constraints of her religion. She feels that this and her high level of confidence carried her through the traumatic periods of her life. Her early start in life as an able-bodied girl would have given her a basic foundation for her confidence. At the time Rosebud became disabled she was already into puberty and her identity as a woman would have started to take shape. She says it took a long time to stop feeling numb but now that she has, she just sees barriers as an exciting challenge in life, which she loves to the full.

Dorothea became disabled after puberty, and her relationship has remained firm. She said,

My partner is wonderful and our relationship is good. We are as much in love as ever. I get quite emotional thinking how good it is. There are just small differences in our sex life. Before I was disabled we used to like going out to make love in the car but although we don't do that now, sex is still good. During love-making, he helps me if I need it.

Safer sex

Issues of safer sex that I raised throughout the interviews have not been highlighted very often by the women themselves. In the survey, 40.88 per cent of disabled women said they did not practise safer sex (see Appendix 3, Fig. 14). One woman commented on her questionnaire, 'I would like to practise safer sex but my boyfriend will not wear a condom.' It is not surprising when sex education in schools is denied us that some disabled women do not practise safer sex.

Crystal talked a little about safer sex in her interview. This was in relation to her university years. When she went to university, her long-standing relationship ended. This was before AIDS and although she took the Pill to avoid pregnancy, this was the only protection she used. She said,

Today I would never dream of sleeping with anybody without condom protection. I came off the Pill years ago so condoms are necessary for me now against pregnancy as well as for protection against AIDS.

Responses to six questionnaires also highlighted the view that some married women did not feel that safer sex was an issue for them as they had a regular partner. As women can never be totally sure what their partner is doing, safer sex is still an issue even in long-standing relationships. Being married is not a reason for not practising safer sex but many women feel it is.

Breaking barriers

Throughout all of the interviews, the disabled women gave accounts of how they started to break down the barriers that they were facing. All strive for empowerment and their accounts depict the different ways that they move towards this. Despite isolation and the odds stacked against them, each made a push down pathways towards her own independence.

Ruby left home after getting married. The marriage did not last but Ruby's lifestyle became even more independent. She said,

> *After my marriage was over, I did start to have more success with other men. By this time she had her own accessible flat and was financially independent, which helped.*

When she had been living with her parents, she had not been able to get in or out of their home without assistance, as the front door was up several steps. Life had changed drastically by this time. Her husband had left the scene, and Ruby started to get involved in Independent Living in earnest. She said,

> *I find that now, as I get older, although I am attractive to the opposite sex, I do not fear the day when I might not be.*

She feels this is because she has had periods of lack of opportunity. If this should happen again, this will not worry her. She still feels that she has had to make compromises in her relationships as the big passions in her life did not come to fruition.

For the past several years Ruby has had a live-in lover. This relationship started when she was at university and continues today, although it has been through its ups and downs. She also has another sexual relationship with a man who lives close by. Ruby explains,

> *Basically, it is hard to get what you need from just one person.*

She prefers this rather precarious balancing act in having two people she is involved with as they both satisfy different needs. Her live-in lover has a lovely sense of humour and her second, new lover gives her the sentimentality that she needs. She went out to seek a new lover to fill a gap and at present is not looking for any more. She does not like to be preoccupied with searching for partners as it is very time-consuming but does not like to be on her own either.

Ruby changed her life around and is today coping with a successful career, lovers and maintaining her own flat. She broke barriers in a big way and has built her own happiness. This is not typical of the majority of disabled women, as the survey has shown that many disabled women are still looking for a sexual relationship. Crystal also broke down barriers within her life and now lives independently but for her it was also a slow start. Crystal gave this account of how life started to change for her.

When she left school, she still had not had a sexual relationship. She then went to a training college in Surrey and from then on life changed drastically. Away from the over-protective environment that her parents had created, Crystal started experimenting with relationships. The first two men she went out with and had sexual relations with turned out to be married. After a few months she started going out with her third boyfriend and became engaged. Although Crystal loved wearing the ring and 'being engaged', she did not want to settle down and eventually broke off the engagement. She said,

It felt too much like losing my freedom just when I had found it.

She then started going out with a man from the college who was some seven years her senior. At this time Crystal was deeply in love. She had loved the freedom that college had offered and was determined that she would find her own place to live.

When Crystal turned 20, she moved away from home. She said,

It was just far enough away from my parents to break loose but near enough for me to go home when I missed them.

She was still working but by the time she got home from work and looked after the flat, she lacked the energy for contact with friends. Crystal recalls that for most of her life she has used up her energy quickly. She suffers from a weak chest and blames this for her lack of energy.

Despite going out very infrequently, she had not been living in her flat for long before she started another sexual relationship. She lived with that partner for six years. Crystal said,

> *I actually lived with him for a year before I told my parents. They were very upset and felt this was a shame on the family.*

However, she resisted marriage as she was not prepared to let her freedom go at all. She recalls how she was very fond of her partner but did not love him deeply and so the relationship jogged along. Crystal said,

> *At that time I felt that living with a man added a statement to my life about my own feelings of freedom, so I rejected marriage.*

Since leaving university, Crystal has had several jobs. Once she was back in the community, her circle of friends shrunk and her relationships stopped altogether again; there was not even a one-night stand in sight. She said,

> *Since I was 28 to when I was 45 the relationships just dried up. I had two flings with married men during this period but in the main I have lived alone. Making relationships is difficult for everybody but for disabled women it is even harder.*

She feels that she only has enough energy to look after herself and this leaves little for forming relationships. The time and effort that are needed to go out socially are too much for her to cope with. Although she lives in a suburb, many of the local social venues are still inaccessible and so the effort to go out can pose a major problem.

Crystal's breaking of barriers has been hampered by her own energy levels. Other disabled women commented on this as being a problem either with their current partners or in searching for new ones. Crystal experiences what many disabled women have cited. Their actual physical impairment can sometimes restrict their relationships just because they become too tired. Crystal says that she prefers to keep her energy for the things she physically needs to do and that to be involved in a relationship requires too much extra effort. She does, however, live independently and although she feels that her life is still limiting, she enjoys the quality she has now, even if she is alone.

Tara also reached and gained independence. Like Crystal she has chosen not to put energies into sexual relationships. She said,

I don't know whether my desire to be celibate is truly coming from me or from the life I have led. Anyway I am happy enough just spending my time the way I want to. My cats, plants and sewing take up all my time, and anyway cats are better for you; they don't let you down.

Tara takes life in the slow lane and enjoys her freedom away from institution life. She maintains her independence and would be loath to ever give that up. Men do not feature in her life but she does admit to having had a crush on Tom Jones! Tara does not know if her life and wish for chastity would have been different if she had lived at home but is content now and does not wish for more at present.

Pandora has had a sexual relationship for many years. Her parents object to her partner as he is West Indian. Pandora stopped taking him home because of her parents' attitude. She is happy with her partner but does not want to live with him. She said,

I am happy the way we are. We are lovers and good friends. Over the years I raised my self-esteem myself and now I feel content.

Tina also does not want a live-in lover. She said,

Sometimes when I am trying to get the shopping out of my car and push myself in carrying it, I wish I had a man around. Otherwise, I would just be happy with a weekend lover. I feel that I need my energies for myself. Relationships take up a lot of energy.

Ellen is now happy living life in the slower lane. She said,

We still have a sexual relationship but when you get older sex is not the most important thing in life. It's the friendship and caring that is important.

Discussion

Ruby has achieved a lot since the days of isolation that she experienced during her boarding school and teenage years at home. She is now very happy with her two relationships. Both Ruby and Sukie managed to find what they wanted in life the second time around. Both women jumped into their first marriages as a means of escape from the boredom and depression which stem from emotional isolation. Sukie is happy with her second marriage and her children, whereas Ruby is happy being childless and has two lovers.

Crystal, on the other hand, managed to go from home life straight into her own flat. She escaped differently and also escaped a marriage proposal. To Crystal, marriage seemed like losing her freedom as she already had designs of fleeing the nest and was not prepared to feel tied down. She did compromise in that she lived with a man for six years even though she was not deeply in love with him. However, Crystal is still hoping to have another full relationship but lack of energy prevents her from scaling the access barriers that are still out there.

The examples of motherhood outlined above can be seen as typical patterns for all women in general. However, they do need to be considered in the light of disability and the existing barriers that disabled women have to cope with. Unlike able-bodied women, these disabled women were never expected to have children. Their parents did not perceive this, nor did their teachers. This is a very different environment for these women to be in. Most cultures expect women to have children at some stage in their lives unless, of course, they are disabled.

Sukie went ahead but was left feeling isolated in child-rearing, being frightened to ask for the help that she needed in case the children were taken away from her. Maria, Miranda, Gloria, Violet, Heaven and Sophie all managed to cope with motherhood but none found it easy. Ruby never wanted children anyway and does not miss not having them. Crystal still dreams of having children but never has enough energy to form a relationship that would support children.

We can imagine how different the lives of disabled women would be if society supported disabled mothers. Sukie highlighted how the media do not give space for disabled mothers, and with schools and parents not sending out positive messages, it is a wonder that disabled women have children at all. If you add to this the difficulties Sukie mentioned of disability organisations not providing crèche facilities for disabled mothers, the going gets tougher by the second. Sukie's holiday experience of no double beds being available within accommodation specifically designed for disabled people emphasises the problems even further. Where does this image leave the view of disabled women and conception? No wonder Crystal found the going so tough that she ran out of time.

Furthermore sex education not being available to all disabled children would have a knock-on effect on mothering. Lack of information at an early age leaves disabled women at a disadvantage in forming and understanding relationships. This, coupled with actual physical barriers of access, loads the dice heavily against disabled women forming sexual relationships at all.

Sukie pointed out how she feels that it is easier for disabled men and this could be because the caring role of women within society can accommodate this much more easily than the idea of a woman being cared for by a man. Sukie feels that some people see her partner as the carer and that he is 'good' to look after her. Ruby and Crystal both felt the impact of relationships being even more difficult for the more disabled woman. Ruby also pointed to the 'body beautiful' culture which, although it affects all women, singles out disabled women for an especially rough deal. The more disabled a woman is, the further away from the 'body beautiful' image she will be.

The cultural shift required to alter the view of women as carers and needing to be beautiful in order to be lovable will take considerable time. The 'new man' image has not been around for long enough to have mass impact and the changes over the last few decades have been slow in coming to fruition. The 'body beautiful' culture remains immersed within the whole structure of society, the media and advertising industry being its most ardent supporters. Although few women ever come into the category of the body beautiful, the image remains persistent.

Rosebud's history was very different. Her isolation started in her teens. Despite many set-backs and let-downs, she managed to get the kind of relationship that she now has. The difference to her of being seen as nubile one minute and not the next still takes her aback. She says that she has few problems now and most of all misses not having become a vet. She seldom thinks back to the boyfriend who left her but at the time of their parting was devastated. For Rosebud even today it is not the changing view of her sexuality that bothers her, although she finds it irritating, but her change of career plan that still leaves her sad.

Tara had felt isolation in her institution but managed to get out because the institution was being closed and the residents were found alternative accommodation. She says that the best thing in life for her is to cuddle her cats. Tara feels that her sexuality is there but she chooses not to use it at all. She says that she has never had positive role models and if we go back to other disabled women's experiences, we can see that there are so few in society anyway.

Ginger, Sammy and Petra experience life very differently from women who have a visible disability but they also have their problems. All three said it was a strain keeping their disabilities hidden and none of them would be happy declaring her disability on a job application form. Although they find it fairly easy to meet potential partners, they are cautious of declaring themselves disabled to potential lovers. Through this pressure they do not feel totally relaxed in their sexuality and tensions make relationships difficult.

Pandora, Dorothea, Ellen, Heaven, Violet, Gloria and Sophie have long-term relationships and despite all the barriers that exist within society, they are living independently and maintaining their loving relationships. Tina, like Crystal, is living alone and is happy.

Conclusions

The disabled women I interviewed experienced similar barriers that reinforced their isolation. Segregated schooling, housing and transport facilities, coupled with lack of access to the environment and poor employment prospects, all have an impact on disabled women's sexuality. Despite these barriers, these women managed to cope and eventually ended up living independently. However, life should not have to consist of 'managed to cope' and 'eventually'. This is what happens when disabled women are expected to cope in a society that does not make allowances for their needs. Their sexual development is either crushed, restricted or denied. If disabled women are to enjoy their sexuality, the barriers to segregation need to be permanently removed. This can only happen through a major change in society so that it starts taking into account the needs of disabled women. The political shift required to end all forms of segregation would enable all disabled women to develop their sexuality to the full.

The sexual health and equality hypotheses – Testing the hypotheses for disabled heterosexual women

1. That sex education for disabled women, particularly those born disabled is inadequate

34.25 per cent of the women in the survey were born disabled. Of these, 13.26 per cent received no sex education. Overall, 42.54 per cent of disabled women received no sex education. These figures are high considering that sex education forms part of the National Curriculum. This hypothesis has been upheld. (See Appendix 3, Fig. 19).

2. That those disabled women who acquired a disability later in life (as opposed to being born disabled) are more likely to be in a sexual relationship or to have had sexual partners

The survey shows that of those women who became disabled between the ages of eleven and 15 years, and between 16 and 20 years, 4.97 per cent were in sexual relationships. Of those women between the ages of 21 and 25 years, 3.87 per cent were in relationships; of those between 26 and 30 years, 4.97 per cent were in relationships; and of those between 31 and 35 years, 4.42 per cent were in relationships. This compares to 3.03 per cent for those born disabled or who acquired a disability before adolescence. The hypothesis is upheld for the 11–35-year group (Appendix 3, Fig. 18).

3. That race and/or religion influences sexual choices

In this survey 32.04 per cent of disabled women said that religion influenced their sexual choices and 37.02 per cent said that ethnic origin influenced their sexual identity. Of these, 77.34 per cent were white (see Appendix 3, Fig. 32) and 75.14 per cent were heterosexual. This hypothesis has been upheld.

4 . That there was a lack of relevant information about sex

46.96 per cent of the women who answered this question want more sex information and of these, 37.02 per cent who wanted more information were heterosexual. Furthermore, Figure 49 in Appendix 3 shows that 58.01 per cent want a safe environment in which to discuss sex further. This proves the hypothesis that disabled women want more sex information as well as having a need to discuss sexuality issues further.

5. That disabled women lack positive role models to increase self-esteem

In this survey 54.14 per cent of disabled women lacked positive role models. Of these, 40.88 per cent of heterosexual women said that they did not have positive disabled role models. In the interviews I conducted, twelve of the women had no positive disabled role models. This hypothesis has been upheld. (See Appendix 3, Fig. 15).

6. That disabled women are more likely to experience sexual abuse

On the issue of sexual abuse, the survey shows that 41.99 per cent of disabled women have experienced sexual abuse by either family members, partners or carers. This is a high percentage of the overall survey and highlights that disabled women are vulnerable. This hypothesis has been upheld. (See Appendix 3, Figs. 8–10).

7. That disabled women do not practise safer sex

In this sample, Appendix 3, Fig. 14 shows that 40.88 per cent of disabled women said they did not practise safer sex. Of these, around 77 per cent were heterosexual. During the interviews that I conducted, four disabled women felt that they did not need to practise safer sex as they were with long-term partners. It is possible that the actual figure for this question would be much higher if other heterosexual women believe that with regular partners there is no need to practise safer sex. This hypothesis has been upheld.

8. That disabled women are reluctant to talk to each other about sex, but will talk to other people about it

The survey shows that 35.36 per cent of disabled women do not talk to each other about sex (see Appendix 3, Fig. 7). Although this survey shows some reticence, overall this hypothesis has not been upheld for heterosexual women (see Appendix 3, Fig. 24 (ii)).

RIDGE WALKING

this
is my life
out here
on this edge.

windy here
a narrow ridge.

often I am scared
have to squeeze my eyes shut
hug myself to the rock
crawl along on all fours
mumbling mantras.
but sometimes I dance the thin line
whirling in the sun
shouting in an arms-up, head-back laugh

this
is my life
out here —
a slim chance,
with steep drops on either side,
but Christ the views
are bloody marvellous.

Char March

Chapter 4

Common issues

Image and invisibility

How do people form their views of disabled women's sexuality? Most who have no direct experience of disability do so in response to the representation of disabled women in the various popular and cultural media, but what has been the role of this imagery and representation in television, films, books and newspapers? For the most part, disabled women have been conspicuous by their absence from these media, and even in those rare instances where they are present, the representation serves mostly to foster and perpetuate negativity and misunderstanding.

Many of the women who participated in the research argued that the reality of their lives is not reflected in the popular media. The questionnaire statistics show that 54.14 per cent of the contributors (see Appendix 3, Fig. 29) feel that they had had no popular role models to aspire to. Disabled women are rarely seen as ordinary people in ordinary walks of life in mainstream television programmes, in cinema or in books. As Deborah Kent writes in her essay 'In Search of a Heroine: Images of Women in Fiction and Drama','When a woman loses the ability to walk, she is also robbed of her sexuality, her intellect and her sense of self'.

Lisa, one of the contributors, who works in the arts expressed similar sentiments:

> The image of non-disabled women is bad enough. They are usually depicted as sex objects who are used to sell everything from icecream and cough lozenges to cars and the majority of ordinary women can never achieve that image even if they do aspire to it, but disabled women come in for especially bad treatment. On those rare occasions when you do see them on television outside the disability programmes, they are usually non-people who only find their reason for living through the identities of others. In fact, everywhere there is the image and stereotype of disabled women as pathetic, passive victims of charity and handouts shadowing some man who purports to love them. They are never their own people with an identity in their own right.

Annie is a working mother who also expressed the wish that disabled women's lives be reflected more accurately in the popular media:

> Those media people seem to have no imagination, which is laughable really because they are supposed to be creative, but it shouldn't take much imagination to portray us more accurately because we are just ordinary people with ordinary

lives just like most other ordinary people. Why can't they just show us or write about us like we really are? We are not all brave super-humans who do wonderful things despite our disabilities or poor pathetic victims who do nothing at all because of them. Most of us are just ordinary people living ordinary lives – in as much as we can.

The misrepresentation of disabled women is exacerbated by the fact that disabled women themselves are often not in a position to challenge these damaging images. Historically they have been shut out from control in those organisations by which much of this imagery is challenged. There are far too few disabled women in the media who have the power to influence and change the *status quo*. There is little opportunity for them to present real and positive images of disabled women and no one else seems capable of talking or willing to take up the challenge. As a result – perhaps with the exception of disability programmes – the misrepresentation and invisibility of disabled women continues throughout the media and society generally.

Only by creating and circulating more imaginative and positive images can we begin to change some of the negative attitudes towards disabled women. At a conference about disabled people in the media, it was argued that *'disabled people should be shown as an ordinary part of life in all forms of representation, not as stereotypes or invisible'*. Hosted by the Integration Alliance and the Save the Children Fund, the conference was to hear that the depiction of disabled people as invisible or one-dimensional served to reinforce the discrimination and isolation that they experience. Similarly, many of the contributors to the SHE uk research argued that disabled women should be shown expressing their sexuality as an ordinary part of life. They should also be shown as having a range of emotions, being in loving relationships and having similar sexual needs to those of non-disabled women.

Untold misery – The silent trauma that is abuse!

What constitutes child sexual abuse and the extent to which it is prevalent in our society have been major concerns of many state agencies over the past five to ten years. Via the media circus, we have witnessed families torn apart as a result of an allegation of sexual abuse. There has been much discussion about the cause and effect of abuse and the consequences of state intervention in the prevention of, or reaction to charges of, abuse. The debate continues, and such arguments as when a 'simple' photograph of a naked child becomes pornography and thus abuse, will no doubt raise passions into the next decade. The vital consequence of this most distressing subject is that abuse has been named and that victims of abuse are finding the courage to speak out about the effects of this damaging crime. Sexual abuse of disabled people seems to be an extremely prevalent problem in contemporary Britain. Although some cases are reported, most remain unknown except to the victim and the offender.

While 'abuse' is something that apparently happens 'out there' to others, there has been a growing awareness that disabled women, like their non-disabled sisters, have been subjected to abuse. Doucette (1986) found that women with a variety of disabilities were one-and-a-half times as likely to have been sexually abused as children as non-disabled women. Considering the present norms for abuse in the general population of 10 per cent of boys and 25 per cent of girls, these figures suggest the rate of sexual abuse is doubled for girls and five times as high for boys who are deaf (Sobsey, 1994). Brookhouser *et al.* (1986) previously reported higher rates of sexual abuse among hearing-impaired children. Although there remain concerns about sample sizes and selection methods, the general finding of increased risk of sexual abuse of disabled girls and women is uniform. As distressing as it has been to listen to disabled women's accounts, we hope that by sharing their secrets, they have experienced increased acknowledgement and belief in themselves which has been healing. Breaking the silence of this taboo has taken enormous courage, and we hope it will remind other women that they are not alone.

The abuse of disabled children, like the abuse of older people, is a damning indictment of the way in which we treat the most vulnerable members of society.

The fact that disabled people experience violence and abuse is also borne out by the Stonewall (the campaigning organisation of lesbians and gay men) survey which found that 35 per cent of lesbians and gay men had suffered attacks. Preliminary results reveal that black and disabled lesbians and gay men suffered the highest level of violence (the statistics were published in 1996).

The SHE study asked women if they had experienced abuse. Of the women who responded 48 per cent stated they had been abused (see Appendix 3, Figs. 8 and 11). Of these 42 per cent stated they had been sexually abused. We believe that these results confirm the unacceptably high incidence of abuse among disabled girls and women.

Abusers were family members, i.e. partners, fathers, brothers and uncles, or close friends of the family. Abusers were care-givers, i.e. homecarers, nurses, teachers and medical or allied professionals. Abusers included the current or former sexual partners of the disabled women. Although the vast majority of abusers were men, a small percentage were women. Most abusers were known to the disabled girl or woman in question but a small percentage (3.31 per cent – see Appendix 3, Fig. 8) were strangers, and assaults included date rape.

Although most of the abuse took place when these women were young girls, some women remained in abusive relationships today. As Elizabeth stated,

> I was seduced by a woman friend, a nurse, who subsequently told me she never consummates her lesbian relationships. She now only occasionally takes me out and only to church. This is not what I want but it is better than nothing.

The theories of abuse and the individual facets of the relationship between victim and offender are many and have not been extensively researched for this phase of the SHE uk study (see Recommendations). However, there is some evidence to suggest that disabled people who are dependent on paid care-givers are more at risk than those cared for within the family. This is probably the case because economic motivation rather than emotional attachment, which inhibits abuse, maintains the contact (Sobsey from Craft).

The circumstances in which these women found themselves, i.e. isolated and dependent, made it easier for the abuse to take place undetected. Their powerlessness resulted in compliance and a passive acceptance of the abuse. Compliance in itself is a problem in that in order to prevent abuse or resist an abuser, a critical level of self-esteem and assertion is required, yet from a very early age disabled girls are taught to be compliant and accept their circumstances.

Reliance on a sole care-giver resulted in the acceptance of behaviour that in other circumstances would be considered cruel and intolerable. As Lee explains,

> After I became disabled my partner of many years slept with another woman. He said he wanted to make love to a woman who could do whatever he wanted and could not imagine the rest of his life with sex limited by my disability. He said he had contemplated paying for sex but these were excuses for his unfaithfulness.

She explains why she remains in the relationship,

> I am eaten up with jealousy and rage, but I need a great deal of care and it is easier coming from him. At the same time I cannot describe how awful it feels to allow a man who insists he loves and must see another woman, to put me to bed, turn me over at night and carry out essential intimate tasks.

The SHE research revealed that 45.30 per cent of women (see Appendix 3, Fig. 46) had difficulty with sex for physical reasons and 30.30 per cent of women stated that disability contributed to the abuse (see Appendix 3, Fig. 13).

Robbed of childhood

The impact and effect of childhood sexual abuse is not to be under-estimated. Some women felt their childhood stopped when they were introduced to the world of adult sexual experience, as Kirsten states:

> I had a very ambivalent attitude to my sexuality, partly because of sexual abuse as a child. That actually took away my childhood and introduced me to the adult world of sex in an unwilling and unpleasant way.

Kay was sexually abused by her older brother and a 'family friend'. She spent most of her childhood in a state of anxiety and depression:

> I wanted people to know, I wanted help but I was terrified to tell ... I had been told to keep this secret. I didn't learn much at school, I spent so much time in a fantasy world, where I was a different little girl, living in a different family ... Because we are told to keep the abuse a secret, we know it's wrong. I used to look at other girls in school and think, 'Does this happen to them?' But I knew I was different. I never felt free, I was always on guard. I hope today, if a child was in my position, that someone, especially a teacher, would notice and do something.

Abuse not only robs the child of freedom and childhood but adds to her sense of alienation and difference. Kirsten says,

> *Sexual abuse totally affected the way I related to myself as a lovable person as this was an act of hatred, lots of acts of hatred born out of a relationship which had been loving, i.e. between my brother and myself.*

The disabled child may well question how lovable she is and ask herself whether this is happening because she is disabled and different. From these accounts, it would appear that whatever the uncertainties before the abuse, the abuse results in confusion, low self-esteem and a feeling of being acutely different.

Abuse as a cause of impairment

Others felt that the effect of childhood sexual abuse had 'caused' their impairment later in life, either directly as a result of bodily harm or indirectly as a consequence of living with painful repressed memories that they could not share. Liz says,

> *I had a boss who made me strip to my panties whenever he called me into his office (at least once a week). This was very humiliating and partially caused my illness and retirement from work.*

Sarah explains how abuse suffered in childhood caused her disability:

> *I am disabled as a result of childhood sexual and physical abuse which caused damage to my spine and brain, although it has taken a long time to get this bad.*

Julie, a mental health system survivor, states,

> *I don't know a woman who has not been subjected to serious harassment, sexual abuse or rape. I have been abused, raped, subjected to incredible violence and I have survived ... but not without going nuts! Incidentally, the last serious assault happened while I was in a mental health clinic.*

Abuse and sexual identity: 'You're only this way because you were abused'

Some lesbians explained that their sexuality was considered deviant by their families, carers or medical professionals. Those who told of the sexual abuse they had suffered were then 'accused' of being frigid or lesbian because of this abuse (lesbianism was equated with hating men rather than loving women). For those women whose impairment is mental distress, this is a particularly harsh judgement which denies them choice over their sexual identity.

Some women who grew up with strong emotional and sexual feelings towards other women were unable to act upon these feelings. They needed to escape from their abusers and took the easiest route out. Gloria, abused throughout her childhood, explains how, although at the time of getting married she did not remember the sexual abuse, she knew she needed to get away from home:

> I was desperate to get out of the house and marriage was the only way out. Because of my cerebral palsy and my low self-esteem I had great reservations about who would have me and how I would have children but I knew somehow I'd manage. I didn't remember the abuse at the time of my marriage at 20, but it had the effect of destroying my image and self-esteem.

Owing to social conditioning and family pressures, many lesbians are under pressure to get married and have unsatisfactory sexual and emotional lives. It seems obvious that if 25 per cent of girls and women are sexually abused, some of these will be lesbians. However, it is important to state that they are not lesbians simply because they were abused or that they hate all men but because they love women. As Sheila states,

> I was sexually abused by my step-father and a 'friend of the family'. I am not a lesbian because I have been abused. I have always known I was a lesbian but due to circumstances, including being disabled and needing support from my family, I could only come out when I felt safe and supported enough to do so.

Conclusion

We were surprised at the high incidence of abuse among the sample of women in our study. As this first study's main objective was to explore the impact of disability on sexuality, the information gathered on abuse is almost incidental. It would appear from women's accounts that economic and physical dependency, plus isolation as a result of impairment, are important contributory factors. However, a further study to examine additional factors that may result in the abuse of disabled girls and women seems of vital importance. We need to know more about the factors resulting in incidents of abuse, the 'socialisation' of disabled girls and women, the relationship between perpetrator and victim, social, economic and environmental factors and the consequences of abuse. This may then enable us to make recommendations about the avoidance of abuse, which, we acknowledge, is damaging to self-esteem, life-threatening and still a nightmare today for many disabled girls and women.

Mothering – issues for all women

The issue of mothering pointed to the many problems that all disabled women face in motherhood. In the SHE survey 29.28 per cent disabled women said that as girls they did not have expectations of getting married and having babies (see Appendix 3, Fig. 20). If able-bodied girls gave this high response, it would be surprising. Of the sample, 58.01 per cent said that they did not have children (see Appendix 3, Fig. 22) but 34.81 per cent said they wanted them (see Appendix 3, Fig. 23). These figures indicate that mothering for disabled women does not go smoothly. There are many criticisms that disabled women have to tolerate in order to experience and enjoy motherhood. During interviews with disabled women on mothering, respondents gave varied examples of the negativity that they had faced.

Do not reproduce yourself

Across society, disabled mothers have felt under pressure to have babies only if they were going to be able-bodied ones. This pressure has come from family and friends. Disabled mothers have been made to feel selfish if they go ahead and have a disabled baby, and at all costs, the baby must be able-bodied. They are constantly under pressure not to reproduce themselves because of their disability.

Miranda recalls,

> *Some people saw me as horrendous, awful and totally immoral for going ahead and having a disabled baby when I had the choice. It is society's way of saying that you must not have disabled children. There is pressure on all women to have perfect babies.*

However, not everybody was so negative and prejudiced. There were some progressive people who supported Miranda's decision to be a mother, as she explains,

> *Some people congratulated me and told me how wonderful it was that I had stretched disabled motherhood past restricting limits. Lizzy, my daughter, has been well loved by many people since she was born and I have never been criticised for my parenting ability. People say that I have done a really good job.*

Sophie said,

When I was pregnant, some people assumed that my baby would also be disabled. I kept telling them that polio was not passed on through my genes but it made no difference. I felt some people only supported me after my child was born and they could see it was able-bodied. My parents breathed a sigh of relief even though they said they did not care whether my child had a disability or not. I really felt a lot of pressure to have an able-bodied child, which I was likely to do anyway.

She has also felt support increase as the years have gone by and says,

My friends today give me a lot of support, and tell me that I have done really well. I know I have but it is good to hear this from other people. If I had had a disabled baby I know things would have worked out in the end. I would never have had an abortion anyway. Why should I? I am disabled and have every right to a full and happy life.

Different expectations

Maria is a blind mother and she, too, had to resist people's prejudice. She said,

When you are disabled, people expect you not to be good at mothering. Even my own mother thought I would not make a very good mother. Now she has to admit that she feels I am better at parenting than my brothers and sisters. I still went ahead and resisted this view because I had always wanted babies. I can remember as a child, I wanted to have babies once I grew up.

What Maria had not expected was the emotional grief that came with her motherhood, which was connected to her disability. She said,

I felt very angry that I could not see my children and other people could. I do believe in the social model of disability but it does not cover all our needs. Also, when I had children I felt I became more disabled. Getting around as a blind person is all right but getting around as a blind woman with children is more difficult. Take the underground, for instance: if you have children with you, life is much more difficult.

Sophie said,

When I was a little girl, I had wanted to have children when I grew up. I did not expect it to be so difficult. My husband was wonderful but many people we knew seemed to think this was the time to give us condolences. It took a lot of doing, but I just ignored them. True friends support you, so we ended up changing a lot of our friends. I am going to have more children though; I have just grown a thicker skin to cope.

Violet has not experienced any particular difficulty with her mothering years. She said,

I had three children – two boys and one girl. My husband is also disabled but we have managed over the years. My children have grown up now and left home. I coped and it was OK. I don't think there is much more I can add, only that if I had my children today, I would expect my life to go the same way, with the two of us coping together. I think our relationship and closeness has been the success in my life.

Lack of help and support

This is a time when disabled women should feel they can get help whenever they need it, but they have experienced both lack of support and fear of asking for help, as Sukie explains,

I was afraid that social services would take my babies away if they thought I could not cope. Life would have been wonderful with extra help when my babies were small. Instead I had to be as able-bodied as possible.

Maria said,

If I had had more help with my children I would not have felt so isolated. For instance, if I had been provided with a driver I would not have felt more disabled but more empowered as a disabled mother. They sent me an awful health visitor with very narrow views about disabled mothers. I have found a lot of health visitors had narrow views on disability. This is really something that I now want to work towards changing.

Sophie also commented,

I did feel very much that I had to get on with things on my own. My family helped a lot, so I suppose I did not feel the pressure so much but if I had not lived near my family, life would have been tough. I don't know how other people manage if they do not have a big family to support and help them.

Mothering skills not being recognised

There is the view that if disabled women are with able-bodied partners, their partners have to do all the coping, as Heaven has experienced,

> *My husband is always getting praised for the children being healthy and happy. You would think that I had nothing to do with this, yet I am the one who is with them all the time. Pat works shifts and does not see them often, yet people think their well-being is all down to him. Another thing: people assume that the children do not get their fair share of trips out but they do. We go out a lot at weekends but I still get comments about them needing to see the world a bit more. My mothering skills are often negated. It is as if other people have already made up their minds and see my life as they want to see it.*

Lesbian women also have their motherhood denied them. Kay explains,

> *As a disabled lesbian, I rarely get validation of my motherhood. Disabled people see me as an 'out' lesbian. Lesbians see me as a disabled dyke. Nobody recognises that the major part of my reason for being, and the thinking behind my decision-making, is the fact that I have three sons at home that I am trying to rear the best way I know how.*

Sophie said,

> *Although my family help a lot, I don't get recognition for the mothering that I do. My husband does give me recognition but not everybody does. It is as if my disability cancels out the mother role that I have. I love my role as a mother and I wish it was given higher status.*

Not allowed to be a mother

Other barriers that disabled mothers face are that they should not be mothers at all. Sara said,

> *People are shocked and wonder whether I should have kids, being lesbian and a crip, but when they see me with my kids, they do change their minds.*

Lesbian mothers also find that sometimes their children have difficulty in coping with their mothers' identity. There is a pressure to be as 'normal' as possible, both sexually and physically. Bee said,

I was in a heterosexual relationship and then I came out as a lesbian. I was open to most people about this but I found that my children did not like it and were hostile and secretive about my new life. They still find it difficult that I am disabled or lesbian.

Gloria experienced resistance to her motherhood from her mother-in-law. She says,

When I first went out with Lenny, I could see his mother disapproved. Lenny was her only son and she did not want him getting hitched to a disabled woman. When I became pregnant, she was definitely not pleased. Now we have two babies, she has mellowed a bit, but there is still a coolness from her. She really had wanted her daughter-in-law to be able-bodied. If my children had also been disabled as well, she really would have freaked out. She really did not want me to be the mother of her grandchildren.

Gloria seems to have handled her mother-in-law's resistance well but her husband found it more difficult. She said,

Lenny felt badly about his mother's reaction. He is still not over it. At the end of the day I didn't really care what anybody thought about my wish to have children. Lenny was really hurt by his mother. She was silly. Her lack of insight hurt her own son, and he still thinks less of her today.

Wealth and gender

When babies are seen as wealth, the problem becomes intensified as black disabled women have experienced. As they are disabled, they are seen as not being able to have babies, yet having lots of babies is seen as a symbol of wealth. Caz explained this pressure:

My mother had a lot of children and this pleased her family. Then I came along and I know that my family do not expect me to have babies because I am disabled. I don't want any at the moment but I am aware that children are connected with the status I will hold, or not as the case might be. I feel that it is impossible for me to say that I don't want babies because I don't want them. It is nothing to do with being disabled.

Others have felt the pressure to produce boys. Pat has five daughters and has not felt valued:

I would change one of my daughters for a boy, if I could.

She is 52 and is still trying for a son.

Kuldip echoed these views,

> *Within my family, I am seen as somebody who needs to be looked after for the rest of my life. They would find it hard to view me as a mother, looking after babies. Within our Asian culture boys are still prized, so if I had lots of baby boys my value as a woman might go up.*

Conclusion

Our research has highlighted some of the difficulties that disabled women have experienced during their mothering years. The amount of resistance that they have had to face in order to have children is incredible. Disabled pregnant women should not have to contend with the kinds of pressures that these women have cited as examples of oppression. There are issues of societal views of discrimination as well as of the cultural norms that need to be resisted. The lack of adequate support from care support agencies also needs to be addressed.

It would be necessary for us to research this subject further in order to ascertain the potential help that could be made available to pregnant disabled women. This would enable us to produce clear recommendations to support agencies as well as to disabled mothers.

Conclusions

The SHE research has shown that the persistent denial or distortion of disabled women's sexuality can have important repercussions which are varied and numerous. For example, the widespread belief that disabled women are asexual inevitably leads to the misconception that they have no interest in or aspirations for sexual and personal relationships. Yet the majority of women in the survey showed that they do share many of the same or similar aspirations as those of their non-disabled counterparts. For example, over 65 per cent of all those who participated in the survey said that, as children, they had expected to grow up to explore and express their sexuality through the establishment of relationships, getting married and having children.

However, the study also shows that disabled women's opportunities to fulfil these aspirations are often not the same as those of their non-disabled contemporaries. Being continually relegated to lesser services, education, jobs and social opportunities all make it extremely difficult for them to develop and explore social contacts and relationships. Significantly, 41.44 per cent of all participants (see Appendix 3, Fig. 21) said that they were not in a sexual relationship though most of them wished to be. In fact, the difficulties and barriers that some disabled women experience can often make sexual relationships extremely difficult for them to consider or achieve. In the worst case scenario, this may result in almost total social isolation with little opportunity to form relationships or explore sexuality. This can in turn result in them being 'infantilised' with a subsequent enforced childlessness as nearly 35 per cent of the contributors testified (see Appendix 3, Fig. 23).

In addition, a lack of appropriate sex education for disabled girls and young women may give rise to a heightened susceptibility to sexual abuse. As the survey shows 29.28 per cent of all the respondents said that they had experienced sexual abuse by a member of their family (see Appendix 3, Fig. 9). This is compared with a reported 25 per cent of non-disabled girls who experienced sexual abuse. A further 24.31 per cent said that they were the victims of sexual abuse by someone other than a family member (see Appendix 3, Fig. 8), while a staggering 48 per cent said that they had suffered other forms of abuse (see Appendix 3, Fig. 11). This, in turn, can have many damaging consequences which may include sexually transmitted diseases, unplanned pregnancy and exposure to the human immunodeficiency virus (HIV).

The research also shows that there are many other issues which are important to disabled women such as abortion, safer sex, the impact of AIDS and HIV, reproduction, sexual dysfunction and a whole host of other topics. Throughout the information gathering many of the women argued that there was an urgent need for more information and resources to help disabled women to understand better and to resolve issues regarding their sexuality. Nearly 47 per cent of the contributors (see Appendix 3, Fig. 28) said that they wanted more sex education and information. Most importantly, they felt that there should be more fora whereby disabled women could come together to support and encourage each other about their sexuality.

However, despite the numerous misunderstandings and barriers, many of the women in the survey are forging for themselves a positive sense of who and what they are. Their lifestyles explode the myth that disabled women are asexual. As they continue to confront some of the dominant assumptions and prevailing prejudices, they have begun to construct more realistic and interesting images of themselves and disabled women generally. In so doing, many have refused to become victims of the prejudice and misunderstandings of others.

Recommendations

The SHE uk research into disabled women's sexuality has raised a number of issues that require further attention. Some of the more painful and distressing issues, such as sexual abuse and damaging isolation, seem too complex to make recommendations about. However, the simple telling of their stories has been healing for most women. While acknowledging the multiplicity of factors that results in incidents of abuse and disempowerment, including the socio-economic climate in which we find ourselves as disabled people in 1990s Britain, we believe there are small but significant steps that will be beneficial today. We shall attempt to list them as recommendations, to provide a basis on which to take this work forward and improve the lot of disabled women everywhere.

Naming the abuse

It has been particularly cathartic for women to tell their stories of abuse – to say out loud that they were abused at the hands of fathers, brothers, husbands, carers, etc. It has often been suggested that people will open up to and share more with those who are like themselves. As disabled women researchers, we have been trusted with the most painful and intimate details of these women's lives. We have acknowledged what they have said, listened attentively and believed their stories. As abuse thrives on inequality and silence, it is important to highlight disabled women's position in society and to name the unacceptable behaviour that is abuse.

Information

As one of our respondents pointed out, non-disabled women can learn about sex from a variety of sources. They can pick up a magazine any week and there will be at least one article on sex and relationships. Turn the TV on and able-bodied, heterosexual people are in romantic encounters, but where can disabled women go to learn about sex or see the reality of their lives reflected?

'Information is power, and disabled women don't have enough of it'

Sex education for all

One thing seems sure: disabled women are sexual beings and would appreciate opportunities to develop their sexual identities, to meet people and to form relationships. The taboos surrounding disabled people and sex seem to be thriving. However, disabled people always have had and will continue to have sexual relations. This being the case, it seems imperative that they receive sex education to prepare them. Sex education should be provided at every opportunity and not something that is done once at school and is based solely on reproduction.

Appropriate sexual health services

Discussion with the Family Planning Association (FPA) and so-called specialist services, such as spinal injury units reveals a history of neglect of sexual health services for disabled women. The FPA has not yet developed a policy regarding services to disabled women. Many local family planning clinics are housed in inaccessible buildings and are inappropriate or insensitive to the needs of disabled women. On contacting spinal injury units, we were informed that sexual health or the return to sexual function after injury was not something they discussed. We found that there was the opportunity to talk to a counsellor, but this was usually an *ad hoc* service for disabled men worried about fatherhood or continuing sexual intercourse with partners.

As women are seen as 'ill' rather than disabled and have the status of life-long patients, they are all too often referred to doctors with problems which are social, environmental, emotional and even financial. As these problems are very often outside the remit of most doctors, disabled women can find themselves being blamed for their problems in the face of professional impotence. One woman was accused of not loving her husband because she found sexual intercourse painful. A second was told that her love for another woman was not real love and referred to a psychiatrist.

Fully accessible services providing relevant information and appropriate sexual health care are not a luxury but a necessity for disabled women.

Being part of the solution – 'user' involvement/user-led services

Disabled women are clear about what they need in order to become fully functioning human beings with healthy sex lives. What they are frustrated about is the fact that no one seems interested in seeking their expertise. The concept of 'user' involvement is well established and forms the basis of most appropriate consultation exercises. The user's view has been sought by professionals and agencies in order to provide services that are both wanted and needed. The same principle should apply to sexual health services with users' needs central to the development of service provision.

There are isolated initiatives where services have arisen out of a perceived need, but these are all too often knee-jerk reactions to unexpected behaviour. For example, one local authority developed a sexuality policy and peer group counselling when it came to light that users with learning difficulties were having sex. More enlightened authorities have contacted their local organisations of disabled people and are developing relevant peer education and counselling initiatives together.

Positive images and role models

Disabled women are in successful relationships, managing careers and households and are rearing healthy, well-adjusted children; yet, they are not reflected in any media other than as the 'plucky, determined or brave cripple'. The reality of disabled women's lives must be represented in the media: we are everywhere and should be seen to be everywhere. As one of our respondents wrote, 'Women's bodies are used to sell anything and everything from soap to cars ... When did you last see an older wrinkled woman or a disabled woman draped across the bonnet of a Jaguar?'

Opportunities to share experiences, fears and hopes

Although some women were reluctant to talk about sex to other women, most stated that they wanted a safe environment in which to discuss intimate problems or concerns. Confidentiality and respect were essential elements of this safe place. We worked within workshops and small groups or on a one-to-one basis. The preference varied, but the need and desire to talk were unanimous. SHE made contact with women from all over the UK and could use these contacts to continue the dialogue with disabled women. The primary aims of workshops would be the sharing of problems and ideas. They would also be important in addressing the damaging isolation experienced by so many disabled women.

Resources for disabled women provided by disabled women

Young disabled women, like their non-disabled peers, should be able to read about sex in any magazine. As this is not, in fact, the case we need to invest in materials which are appropriate, relevant and accessible. Disabled women require information about relationships, pregnancy and mothering, sexual practice, sexually transmitted diseases, including HIV, and about managing change; information that will educate them and keep them safe. A database, a resource list and a sexual health library developed for and by disabled women are also required. *Information is power and it saves lives.*

References

Brookhouser *et al.* (1986), quoted in Craft A (ed.). *Sexuality and Learning Disabilities*. London: Routledge, 1994.

Disability in the Media: Save the Children publication sales, 17 Grove Lane, London SE5 8RD.

Doucette (1986), quoted in Craft A (ed.). *Sexuality and Learning Disabilities*. London: Routledge, 1994.

Kent D (1988). 'In Search of a Heroine: Images of Women with Disabilities in Fiction and Drama', *Women with Disabilities: Essays in Psychology, Culture and Politics*, Temple University Press.

Sobsey D (1994), quoted in Craft A (ed.). *Sexuality and Learning Disabilities*. London: Routledge, 1994.

Appendix 1

Disabled women's seminar

This seminar was held on 19 August 1995, at the London Women's Centre, Wesley House, London WC2, and presented the results of the SHE uk's sexuality questionnaire project to disabled women.

Women who had returned the questionnaire indicating that they were interested in follow-up meetings were invited to hear the results and voice their views on work covered to date. Women came from both London and the provinces. Thirty disabled women were invited, and 19 attended; of these the largest group consisted of lesbian and bisexual women, followed by women from the heterosexual group. Black women were in the minority.

The opening seminar discussed the background to the research and the dearth of research that is available around issues on the sexuality of disabled women. During this opening presentation different initial reactions to this research were also explored. At the start of the project, these ranged from comments that had suggested it was not 'sexy' enough, to men ringing up complaining that questionnaires had been sent to their wives!

The conclusions to the opening session acknowledged that, as this was the first research of its kind, further research was needed to cover areas such as abuse and safer sex. In this project 1,000 questionnaires were sent out through both organisations for disabled people and those controlled by disabled people, and through institutions, women's groups, trade unions and some social services departments. The mailing list consisted of some 200 organisations.

SHE uk sent the questionnaires through organisations to maintain confidentiality. We have not been able to ascertain how many of the 1,000 questionnaires reached disabled women, as we know that at least three organisations did not send them out. One claimed that none of its members was interested in sex, the second said that it did not have any lesbians or people from black groups so it would not participate, and a third returned the questionnaires to SHE uk over a year-and-a-half later apologising for having missed the deadline.

At the beginning of the project we spent time talking to the advisers from the disability movement on heterosexual, lesbian and race issues in regard to the content of the questionnaire. After preliminary discussion with women representing different parts of the movement, we tested the questionnaire on a pilot group. We then incorporated their comments into the questionnaire (e.g. one section was added for disabled women to describe their disability). SHE uk was now ready to run the full project.

Discussion of results

Out of the 1,000 questionnaires that were sent out we received 181 back. The answers to the questionnaires were collated on Excel (a spreadsheet package) and cross-tab data results and graphs were presented to the disabled women at the seminar.

It was noted that the largest group to reply via the questionnaires were heterosexual women. The second largest group were lesbian and bisexual women. The smallest group were black women. The problems that arose in reaching lesbian, bisexual and black groups were explored and discussed. Although heterosexual women were the largest group of respondents, they were not represented in the same way at the seminar (the largest group being lesbian and bisexual women). Ethnic minority groups were also under represented both on the questionnaire and at the seminar. It was felt that lesbian women were far more experienced at coming out and making their voices heard on issues of sexuality than black and heterosexual women. The seminar took place in London during the school holidays, which might have influenced the turnout of disabled women.

Presentation of results

Pivot tables and graphs presented to the seminar included:

- Ethnic Identity *by* Age
- Class *by* Age
- Sexual Identity *by* Culture
- Born Disabled *by* Sexual Identity
- Born Disabled *by* Expected to get Pregnant
- Sexual Identity *by* Religion
- Age *by* Sexual Identity
- Class *by* Sex Education

- Age *by* Abort Unborn Child with Impairment
- Other Abuse *by* Abused by Carer
- Other Abuse *by* Abused by Family
- Other Abuse *by* Abused by Other
- Sexual Abuse *by* Abused by Carer
- Sexual Abuse *by* Abused by Family
- Sexual Abuse *by* Abused by Other
- Practise Safer Sex *by* Understand Safer Sex

After exploring the results of the questionnaire, the seminar made the following recommendations:

Recommendations – the way forward

- That SHE uk do some future in-depth work on physical and sexual abuse. It was agreed that self-help leaflets to assist survivors of abuse specific to the needs of disabled women be developed and distributed widely.

- That a newsletter be produced in order to help isolated women keep in contact with each other.

- That a SHE Network be established across the country which would cover issues such as reproductive rights and empowerment and provide a social connection.

- That more information on sexuality be distributed to disabled women.

- That another questionnaire be drawn up to ascertain how isolated women could best be supported.

- That a video pack on disabled women's sexuality would be helpful.

- That a good-practice guide on sexuality, written by disabled women, be produced for care support agencies.

- That information leaflets be produced about disabled women and relationships.

- That a safer sex guide for disabled women be produced.

- That a counselling service run by disabled women be launched.

- That more sex education be provided in schools for younger disabled women and children. General sex education should include disability issues as a matter of course.

- That disabled women be encouraged to discuss and support each other through small group discussion sessions aimed at raising self-esteem and combating disempowerment.

Follow-up resources

The seminar ended with a discussion about how vast the needs are that had been highlighted by the SHE questionnaire. While this is the first questionnaire of its kind it was felt that further research and information dissemination would need to follow. Women commented on how disabled women need time to get to grips with redefining their own sexuality and the difficulties that arise within a society that sees the majority of them as asexual.

Obviously projects of the size that the recommendations are suggesting will take time and funders will have to be found either from Europe or within the UK. SHE uk has been growing with women continuing to contact the researchers through the questionnaire, through their organisations and as individuals. It has generated interest and debate which will prove fruitful for all disabled women. Copies of the questionnaire continue to be returned and disabled women are still asking for copies. The questionnaire project could be continuous.

Appendix 2

The questionnaire

Confidential

Please read the following questions carefully and answer to the best of your recollections and/or feelings. **Remember** this questionnaire and its contents will remain confidential

About me ...

1.   Age........
2.   Ethnic Origin........
3.   Religion..........
4.   Culture....................
5.   Place of birth...........
6.   Area of residence: City or rural...........
7.   Sexual Identity : Lesbian/heterosexual/bisexual?.............
8.   What social class do you consider yourself to be? ....
9.   Were you educated in a special school? ....
10.   At what age did you leave school? ....
11.   Did you obtain any qualifications? ....
12.   Did you receive higher education? ....

About my race, religion, culture...

13.   Has your religion shaped or influenced your sexual identity?..........
14.   Has your culture shaped or influenced your sexual identity?...........
15.   Did your family ever contemplate an arranged marriage for you?........
16.   Are you in an arranged marriage?..........
17.   Was the arranged marriage considered only with a disabled person?.....
18.   Was your marriage arranged with your consent?...........
19.   Did your disability influence your eligibility for an arranged marriage?..........
20.   Has the arranged marriage influenced your sexual fulfilment?...........
21.   Has your religion or culture influenced the expression of your sexual choices?...........
22.   Was there any pressure on you to make a choice?........

23. Was there the same expectations of you to do with religion, culture and custom as your able-bodied sisters or peers?........

About how I spend my time...

24. Are you employed?............
25. Were you ever expected to go out to work?.......
26. How long have you been employed?............
27. If you are unemployed do you attend a day centre or stay at home?........

About growing up...

28. Were you born disabled?............
29. At what age did you become disabled?............
30. Are there other disabled members in your family?...........
31. At what age did you start having sexual feelings?...........
32. Did you receive sex education?..............
33. At what age did you receive sex education?..........
34. From whom did you receive sex education, e.g. teacher/parent?..........
35. As a child, did you have ideas about relationships?.............
36. As a child, did you expect to have a life partner?............
37. As a child, did you expect to marry and have children?...........
38. Did your parents/teachers have expectations of you having relationships/getting married?..........

About romance and sexual feelings...

39. At what age did you have your first romantic friendship?...........
40. At what age did you have your first sexual friendship?.............
41. When did you first masturbate/engage in solitary sex?.............
42. Have you had a full sexual relationship?.............
43. Were your sexual relationships heterosexual, lesbian or both?..........
44. Were your partners disabled, able-bodied or both?...........
45. Where do you meet friends/partners, club, pub, work, other?.............

My identity...

46. As a child did you 'feel' like a girl?...........
47. As an adult do you 'feel' like a woman?.............

48. Do you identify with women's issues?.............

49. Have you been in the role of 'the other woman'?...........

50. Is the role of the other woman usually the only one offered?.........

About relationships...

51. Do you have a partner?..............

52. Does your partner have a disability?.........

53. Is the reaction to your able-bodied partner positive or negative from your family/friends?...............

54. Is the reaction to your disabled partner positive or negative, from your family/friends?...........

55. Are you currently in a sexual relationship?............

56. Would you like to be in a sexual relationship now?........

57. How many sexual partners have you had?...........

58. Do you use contraception?..............

59. Are there any difficulties in obtaining contraception?............

60. Do you practise safe sex?.............

61. Are you clear about what safe sex is?...........

62. Are you comfortable with your body?............

63. Are there any physical reasons resulting from your impairment that make sex difficult e.g. use of catheter?.........

64. Do you know of other women who make love with catheters or colostomies?.........

65. Have you ever been rejected by a lover because of the use of a catheter etc.?.....

Sex talk and information...

66. Would you appreciate more information about sex?............

67. Have you been able to understand information about sex?...........

68. Do you discuss sex with disabled women friends?...........

69. Do you join in sex talk with able-bodied women?...........

70. Would you like the opportunity to discuss sex in a safe environment?...........

71. Would you participate in small group discussion about sex?........

72. Would you require information/discussion about sex on a one-to-one basis?......

73. Did you have positive disabled role models?........

74.   Were you actively discouraged from having sex on account of your impairment?...........

75.   Were your sexual feelings ever ridiculed because of your impairment?

76.   Do you have sexual fantasies?.............

77.   At what age did your fantasies start?........

78.   In your sexual fantasies, do you and/or your partner have an impairment?.............

79.   Do you enjoy fantasies more than having sex?........

80.   Do you use any sex toys/aids?.............

81.   Is this to assist having sex due to impairment?.............

82.   Do you require personal assistance (practical help from a carer) when having sex?..........

83.   Who assists you with sex, are they paid helpers, family members or friends/volunteers?.........

84.   Is this arrangement satisfactory?..........

Reproductive rights...

85.   Do you have children?..........

86.   Do you want children?...........

87.   Were you ever expected to get pregnant?.....

88.   Have you ever had an abortion?......

89.   Were you ever pressurised into having an abortion by the medical profession/partner/family?...........

90.   Did the medical profession support your pregnancy?.........

91.   Did your family support your pregnancy?..........

92.   Did your partner support your pregnancy?........

93.   Have you ever wanted to adopt children?.........

94.   What reaction did you receive from family/friends/adoption agencies?...........

95.   Were you told not to have children?.............

96.   Were there any medical reasons for the previous statement?.............

97.   If your unborn child had an impairment, would you want an abortion?.......

98.   Would you consider being a single parent?.........

Abuse...

99.   Have you been sexually abused at any time?...........

100. Have you experienced other abuse?........

101. Was the abuser your carer, family, other?...........
102. Did being a disabled woman contribute to the abuse?.................
103. Have you sought advice or counselling from any agency?..............
104. Was the advice/counselling appropriate as a disabled woman?.......
105. Are you comfortable with your ability to express your sexuality?...........
106. How would you rate your confidence?

	Low	Moderate	High
at work	....	....	....
at home	....	....	....
with your lover	....	....	....
socialising	....	....	....

Describe your disability...
....

Name and Address (optional)
....
....
....
....
....
....

(Fill in this section if you want information on the forthcoming sexuality conferences and/or want to participate in follow-up interviews)

Please return the completed questionnaire to SHE uk

Statistics

Fig. 1 Age of disabled women by class

Age	Working	Middle	Upper	Other	Not Answered	Grand Total
				Class		
16-20	0.00%	1.10%	0.00%	0.00%	0.00%	1.10%
21-25	2.21%	5.52%	0.00%	0.00%	0.55%	8.29%
26-30	4.42%	7.73%	0.00%	0.55%	1.66%	14.36%
31-35	8.29%	9.39%	0.00%	0.00%	1.10%	18.78%
36-40	8.84%	6.63%	0.00%	0.00%	0.00%	15.47%
41-45	6.63%	11.60%	0.00%	0.55%	0.55%	19.34%
46-50	2.76%	8.29%	0.55%	1.10%	0.55%	13.26%
51-55	1.66%	1.66%	0.00%	0.00%	2.21%	5.52%
56-60	1.10%	0.55%	0.00%	0.00%	0.00%	1.66%
61-65	0.00%	1.10%	0.00%	0.00%	0.00%	1.10%
66-70	0.55%	0.00%	0.00%	0.00%	0.00%	0.55%
71-75	0.00%	0.55%	0.00%	0.00%	0.00%	0.55%
Grand Total	**36.46%**	**54.14%**	**0.55%**	**2.21%**	**6.63%**	**100.00%**

Fig. 2 Sex education according to class

Class	Sex Education					
	Little	N/A	No	Yes	Not Answered	Grand Total
Working	0.00%	0.00%	17.13%	18.78%	0.55%	36.46%
Middle	2.21%	0.55%	20.44%	30.39%	0.55%	54.14%
Upper	0.00%	0.00%	0.55%	0.00%	0.00%	0.55%
Other	0.55%	0.00%	1.10%	0.55%	0.00%	2.21%
No Answer	0.55%	0.00%	3.31%	2.21%	0.55%	6.63%
Grand Total	**3.31%**	**0.55 %**	**42.54%**	**51.93%**	**1.66%**	**100.00%**

Fig. 2b Sex education according to ethnic origin

Ethnic Origin	Sex Education					
	Not Answered	Little	N/A	No	Yes	Grand Total
African	0.00%	0.00%	0.00%	0.55%	0.55%	1.10%
Asian	0.00%	0.00%	0.00%	1.10%	1.10%	2.21%
Black British	0.00%	0.00%	0.00%	0.00%	2.21%	2.21%
Caribbean	0.00%	0.55%	0.00%	1.10%	1.10%	2.76%
Irish	0.00%	0.00%	0.00%	4.42%	1.10%	5.52%
Not Answered	0.00%	0.55%	0.00%	4.42%	5.52%	10.50%
Other	0.00%	0.00%	0.00%	2.21%	1.66%	3.87%
White	1.66%	2.21%	0.55%	28.73%	38.67%	71.82%
Grand Total	**1.66%**	**3.31%**	**0.55%**	**42.54%**	**51.93%**	**100.00%**

Fig. 3 Ethnic origin by age

| | Sex Education | | | | | |
Ethnic Origin	Not Answered	Little	N/A	No	Yes	Grand Total
African	0.00%	0.00%	0.00%	0.55%	0.55%	1.10%
Asian	0.00%	0.00%	0.00%	1.10%	1.10%	2.21%
Black British	0.00%	0.00%	0.00%	0.00%	2.21%	2.21%
Caribbean	0.00%	0.55%	0.00%	1.10%	1.10%	2.76%
Irish	0.00%	0.00%	0.00%	4.42%	1.10%	5.52%
Not Answered	0.00%	0.55%	0.00%	4.42%	5.52%	10.50%
Other	0.00%	0.00%	0.00%	2.21%	1.66%	3.87%
White	1.66%	2.21%	0.55%	28.73%	38.67%	71.82%
Grand Total	**1.66%**	**3.31%**	**0.55%**	**42.54%**	**51.93%**	**100.00%**

Fig. 4 Age by sexual identity

| | Sexual Identity | | | |
Age	Heterosexual	Lesbian	Bisexual	Grand Total
16-20	0.55%	0.55%	0.00%	1.10%
21-25	7.73%	0.00%	0.55%	8.29%
26-30	8.29%	3.31%	2.76%	14.36%
31-35	13.26%	2.21%	3.31%	18.78%
36-40	11.05%	3.87%	0.55%	15.47%
41-45	15.47%	2.21%	1.66%	19.34%
46-50	10.50%	1.10%	1.66%	13.26%
51-55	5.52%	0.00%	0.00%	5.52%
56-60	1.10%	0.00%	0.55%	1.66%
61-65	1.10%	0.00%	0.00%	1.10%
66-70	0.55%	0.00%	0.00%	0.55%
71-75	0.00%	0.55%	0.00%	0.55%
Grand Total	**75.14%**	**13.81%**	**11.05%**	**100.00%**

Fig. 5 Culture by sexual identity

Culture	Sexual Identity			Grand Total
	Bisexual	Heterosexual	Lesbian	
African	0.55%	1.10%	0.55%	2.21%
Asian	0.55%	1.66%	0.00%	2.21%
Black British	0.00%	0.55%	0.00%	0.55%
British UK	6.63%	29.83%	2.76%	39.23%
Caribbean	0.00%	0.55%	0.00%	0.55%
Disabled	0.55%	1.10%	1.10%	2.76%
Irish	0.00%	1.66%	0.55%	2.21%
Jewish	0.55%	0.00%	1.10%	1.66%
Not Answered	1.10%	27.07%	4.42%	32.60%
Other	1.10%	11.60%	3.31%	16.02%
Grand Total	**11.05%**	**75.14%**	**13.81%**	**100.00%**

Fig. 6 Culture of women according to class

Culture	Class					
	Working	Middle	Upper	Other	Not Answered	Grand Total
Other	14	12	1	1	1	29
Not Answered	21	33	0	1	4	59
African	1	1	0	0	2	4
Asian	2	2	0	0	0	4
Black British	0	0	0	1	0	1
British UK	20	45	0	1	5	71
Caribbean	1	0	0	0	0	1
Disabled	3	2	0	0	0	5
Irish	2	2	0	0	0	4
Jewish	2	1	0	0	0	3
Grand Total	**66**	**98**	**1**	**4**	**12**	**181**

Fig. 7 Discuss sex with other disabled women according to class

Class	No	Not Answered	Sometimes	Yes	Grand Total
Working	11.05%	0.00%	2.21%	23.20%	36.46%
Middle	18.78%	1.10%	3.31%	30.94%	54.14%
Upper	0.55%	0.00%	0.00%	0.00%	0.55%
Not Answered	3.87%	0.00%	0.00%	2.76%	6.63%
Other	1.10%	0.00%	0.00%	1.10%	2.21%
Grand Total	**35.36%**	**1.10%**	**5.52%**	**58.01%**	**100.00%**

Fig. 8 Sexual abuse by non-family members

Sexual Abuse	Abuser									
	Friends	Medical Professionals	N/A	No	Not Ans	Other Professionals	Partners	Strangers	Yes	Grand Total
No	0.55%	3.31%	35.91%	2.21%	3.31%	0.55%	1.66%	1.10%	5.52%	54.14%
Not Answered	0.00%	0.00%	0.00%	0.00%	2.21%	0.00%	0.55%	0.00%	0.55%	3.31%
Not sure	0.00%	0.00%	0.00%	0.00%	0.00%	0.00%	0.55%	0.00%	0.00%	0.55%
Yes	2.76%	1.10%	12.71%	2.21%	0.00%	1.10%	1.66%	2.21%	18.23%	41.99%
Grand Total	**3.31%**	**4.42%**	**48.62%**	**4.42%**	**5.52%**	**1.66%**	**4.42%**	**3.31%**	**24.31%**	**100.00%**

Fig. 9 Sexual abuse by family members

Sexual Abuse	Abuser							
	Husband	N/A	No	Not Answered	Partners	Yes	Relatives	Grand Total
Not Answered	0.00%	1.10%	0.00%	2.21%	0.00%	0.00%	0.00%	3.31%
No	1.10%	40.33%	1.66%	3.31%	0.00%	7.73%	0.00%	54.14%
Not sure	0.00%	0.00%	0.00%	0.00%	0.00%	0.55%	0.00%	0.55%
Yes	2.21%	15.47%	1.10%	0.00%	1.10%	20.99%	1.10%	41.99%
Grand Total	**3.31%**	**56.91%**	**2.76%**	**5.52%**	**1.10%**	**29.28%**	**1.10%**	**100.00%**

Fig. 10 Sexual abuse by carer

Sexual Abuse	N/A	No	Not Answered	Yes	Grand Total
No	44.75%	2.21%	3.31%	3.87%	54.14%
Not Answered	1.10%	0.00%	2.21%	0.00%	3.31%
Not sure	0.55%	0.00%	0.00%	0.00%	0.55%
Yes	36.46%	0.55%	0.00%	4.97%	41.99%
Grand Total	**82.87%**	**2.76%**	**5.52%**	**8.84%**	**100.00%**

Fig. 11 Other forms of abuse by non-family members

	Abuser									
Abuse	N/A	No	Not Ans	Strangers	Yes	Medical Professionals	Other Professionals	Partners	Friends	Grand Total
N/A	1.66%	0.55%	0.00%	0.55%	0.00%	0.00%	0.00%	0.00%	0.00%	2.76%
No	29.28%	2.76%	0.00%	0.55%	6.08%	0.55%	0.55%	0.55%	0.55%	40.88%
Not Answered	0.55%	0.55%	5.52%	0.00%	1.10%	0.00%	0.00%	0.00%	0.55%	8.29%
Yes	17.13%	0.55%	0.00%	2.21%	17.13%	3.87%	1.10%	3.87%	2.21%	48.07%
Grand Total	**48.62%**	**4.42%**	**5.52%**	**3.31%**	**24.31%**	**4.42%**	**1.66%**	**4.42%**	**3.31%**	**100.00%**

Fig. 13iii) Class by was the counselling appropriate as a disabled woman

Class	N/A	No	Not Answered	Yes	Grand Total
Working	38	11	4	13	66
Middle	58	16	9	15	98
Upper	1	0	0	0	1
Other	1	1	0	2	4
Not Answered	6	3	2	1	12
Grand Total	**104**	**31**	**15**	**31**	**181**

Fig.14 The sexual identity of women who practise safer sex

Practise Safer Sex	Sexual Identity			Grand Total
	Heterosexual	Lesbian	Bisexual	
Not Answered	9.94%	0.00%	1.66%	11.60%
N/A	7.18%	1.10%	1.10%	9.39%
No	30.94%	6.08%	3.87%	40.88%
Sometimes	1.10%	1.10%	0.55%	2.76%
Yes	25.97%	5.52%	3.87%	35.36%
Grand Total	**75.14%**	**13.81%**	**11.05%**	**100.00%**

Fig. 14b Ethnic origin of women who practise safer sex

Ethnic Origin	Not Answered	N/A	No	Sometimes	Yes	Grand Total
African	0.55%	0.00%	0.00%	0.00%	0.55%	1.10%
Asian	0.55%	0.00%	0.55%	0.00%	1.10%	2.21%
Black British	0.55%	0.00%	0.55%	0.55%	0.55%	2.21%
Caribbean	0.00%	0.00%	0.00%	0.00%	2.76%	2.76%
Irish	1.10%	0.00%	3.31%	0.00%	1.10%	5.52%
Not Answered	1.10%	0.00%	6.08%	0.00%	3.31%	10.50%
Other	0.00%	0.00%	0.55%	1.10%	2.21%	3.87%
White	7.73%	9.39%	29.83%	1.10%	23.76%	71.82%
Grand Total	**11.60%**	**9.39%**	**40.88%**	**2.76%**	**35.36%**	**100.00%**

Fig. 15 Positive disabled role models according to sexual identity

Sexual Identity	Don't Know	N/A	No	Not Answered	Yes	Grand Total
Heterosexual	1.66%	0.55%	40.88%	4.97%	27.07%	75.14%
Lesbian	0.00%	0.55%	7.18%	0.00%	6.08%	13.81%
Bisexual	0.00%	0.00%	6.08%	2.21%	2.76%	11.05%
Grand Total	**1.66%**	**1.10%**	**54.14%**	**7.18%**	**35.91%**	**100.00%**

Fig. 16 Sexual identity of women wanting more sex information

Sexual Identity	Don't Know	N/A	No	Not Answered	Yes	Grand Total
Bisexual	0.55%	0.55%	6.63%	0.55%	2.76%	11.05%
Heterosexual	0.55%	0.00%	34.25%	3.31%	37.02%	75.14%
Lesbian	0.00%	0.00%	5.52%	1.10%	7.18%	13.81%
Grand Total	**1.10%**	**0.55%**	**46.41%**	**4.97%**	**46.96%**	**100.00%**

Fig. 17 Does religion influence sexual choices

Religion	N/A	No	Not Answered	Yes	Grand Total
Buddhist	0.00%	0.00%	0.55%	0.00%	0.55%
Christian	3.31%	32.04%	9.94%	20.99%	66.30%
Hindu	0.00%	0.00%	0.00%	1.10%	1.10%
Muslim	0.00%	0.55%	0.00%	0.00%	0.55%
Jewish	0.00%	0.55%	0.55%	0.00%	1.10%
N/A	0.55%	0.00%	0.00%	1.66%	2.21%
None	1.10%	6.08%	2.21%	5.52%	14.92%
Not answered	2.21%	2.21%	1.66%	1.66%	7.73%
Other	0.00%	1.66%	2.76%	1.10%	5.52%
Grand Total	**7.18%**	**43.09%**	**17.68%**	**32.04%**	**100.00%**

Fig. 18 Age of becoming disabled and in a sexual relationship

Age	No	Not Answered	Yes	Grand Total
0-5	7.18%	0.00%	3.31%	10.50%
6-10	1.66%	0.00%	2.76%	4.42%
11-15	1.66%	0.00%	4.97%	6.63%
16-20	2.76%	0.00%	4.97%	7.73%
21-25	3.31%	0.00%	3.87%	7.18%
26-30	4.97%	0.00%	4.97%	9.94%
31-35	2.21%	0.00%	4.42%	6.63%
36-40	2.21%	0.00%	2.76%	4.97%
41-45	0.55%	0.55%	0.55%	1.66%
46-50	0.55%	0.00%	1.66%	2.21%
51-55	0.55%	0.00%	0.00%	0.55%
56-60	0.55%	0.00%	0.55%	1.10%
Gradual	0.55%	0.00%	0.00%	0.55%
N/A	13.81%	1.10%	18.78%	33.70%
Not Answered	0.55%	0.00%	1.66%	2.21%
Grand Total	**43.09%**	**1.66%**	**55.25%**	**100.00%**

Fig. 19 Born disabled by whether they received sex education

Born Disabled	Little	N/A	No	Not Answered	Yes	Grand Total
No	2.21%	0.55%	28.73%	1.10%	32.04%	64.64%
Not Answered	0.00%	0.00%	0.55%	0.00%	0.55%	1.10%
Yes	1.10%	0.00%	13.26%	0.55%	19.34%	34.25%
Grand Total	**3.31%**	**0.55%**	**42.54%**	**1.66%**	**51.93%**	**100.00%**

Fig. 19b Ethnic origin by born disabled and whether they received sex education

Born Disability	Sex Education	Other	Not Ans	African	Asian	Black British	Caribbean	Irish	White	Grand Total
						Ethnic Origin				
Not Answered	No	0.00%	0.00%	0.00%	0.00%	0.00%	0.00%	0.00%	0.55%	0.55%
	Yes	0.00%	0.00%	0.00%	0.00%	0.00%	0.00%	0.00%	0.55%	0.55%
Not Answered Total		**0.00%**	**0.00%**	**0.00%**	**0.00%**	**0.00%**	**0.00%**	**0.00%**	**1.10%**	**1.10%**
No	Not Answered	0.00%	0.00%	0.00%	0.00%	0.00%	0.00%	0.00%	1.10%	1.10%
	Little	0.00%	0.55%	0.00%	0.00%	0.00%	0.55%	0.00%	1.10%	2.21%
	N/A	0.00%	0.00%	0.00%	0.00%	0.00%	0.00%	0.00%	0.55%	0.55%
	No	1.66%	3.31%	0.00%	0.55%	0.00%	1.10%	2.21%	19.89%	28.73%
	Yes	1.66%	4.42%	0.55%	1.10%	1.66%	0.55%	0.55%	21.55%	32.04%
No Total		**3.31%**	**8.29%**	**0.55%**	**1.66%**	**1.66%**	**2.21%**	**2.76%**	**44.20%**	**64.64%**
Yes	Not Answered	0.00%	0.00%	0.00%	0.00%	0.00%	0.00%	0.00%	0.55%	0.55%
	Little	0.00%	0.00%	0.00%	0.00%	0.00%	0.00%	0.00%	1.10%	1.10%
	No	0.55%	1.10%	0.55%	0.55%	0.00%	0.00%	2.21%	8.29%	13.26%
	Yes	0.00%	1.10%	0.00%	0.00%	0.55%	0.55%	0.55%	16.57%	19.34%
Yes Total		**0.55%**	**2.21%**	**0.55%**	**0.55%**	**0.55%**	**0.55%**	**2.76%**	**26.52%**	**34.25%**
Grand Total		**3.87%**	**10.50%**	**1.10%**	**2.21%**	**2.21%**	**2.76%**	**5.52%**	**71.82%**	**100.00%**

Fig. 20 Class of women who, as children, expected to marry and have babies

Class	Don't Know	No	Not Answered	Yes	Grand Total
Working	0.00%	11.05%	0.55%	24.86%	36.46%
Middle	2.76%	15.47%	1.10%	34.81%	54.14%
Upper	0.00%	0.00%	0.00%	0.55%	0.55%
Other	0.55%	0.00%	0.00%	1.66%	2.21%
Not Answered	0.00%	2.76%	0.55%	3.31%	6.63%
Grand Total	**3.31%**	**29.28%**	**2.21%**	**65.19%**	**100.00%**

Fig. 21 Women in a sexual relationship according to class

Class	No	Not Answered	Yes	Grand Total
Working	13.26%	0.00%	23.20%	36.46%
Middle	23.20%	0.55%	30.39%	54.14%
Upper	0.55%	0.00%	0.00%	0.55%
Other	1.10%	0.55%	0.55%	2.21%
Not Answered	3.31%	0.55%	2.76%	6.63%
Grand Total	**41.44%**	**1.66%**	**56.91%**	**100.00%**

Fig. 22 Women having children according to class

Class	No	Not Answered	Yes	Grand Total
Working	19.34%	0.55%	16.57%	36.46%
Middle	34.81%	1.10%	18.23%	54.14%
Upper	0.55%	0.00%	0.00%	0.55%
Other	0.00%	0.00%	2.21%	2.21%
Not Answered	3.31%	0.00%	3.31%	6.63%
Grand Total	**58.01%**	**1.66%**	**40.33%**	**100.00%**

Fig. 23 Count of class by women wanting children

Class	Don't Know	N/A	No	Not Answered	Too late	Yes	Grand Total
Working	1.66%	9.39%	7.18%	3.31%	0.00%	14.92%	36.46%
Middle	1.10%	13.26%	19.89%	2.76%	0.55%	16.57%	54.14%
Upper	0.00%	0.00%	0.55%	0.00%	0.00%	0.00%	0.55%
Other	0.00%	1.10%	0.00%	0.00%	0.00%	1.10%	2.21%
Not Answered	0.00%	2.76%	1.10%	0.00%	0.55%	2.21%	6.63%
Grand Total	**2.76%**	**26.52%**	**28.73%**	**6.08%**	**1.10%**	**34.81%**	**100.00%**

Fig. 24i) Sexual identity of women who discuss sex with other disabled women

Sexual Identity	No	Not Answered	Sometimes	Yes	Grand Total
Heterosexual	26.52%	0.55%	4.97%	43.09%	75.14%
Lesbian	3.87%	0.55%	0.55%	8.84%	13.81%
Bisexual	4.97%	0.00%	0.00%	6.08%	11.05%
Grand Total	**35.36%**	**1.10%**	**5.52%**	**58.01%**	**100.00%**

Fig. 24ii) Sexual identity of women who discuss sex with able-bodied women

Sexual Identity	No	Not Answered	Sometimes	Yes	Grand Total
Heterosexual	17.68%	0.55%	3.31%	53.59%	75.14%
Lesbian	1.66%	0.00%	0.55%	11.60%	13.81%
Bisexual	1.66%	0.00%	0.00%	9.39%	11.05%
Grand Total	**20.99%**	**0.55%**	**3.87%**	**74.59%**	**100.00%**

Fig. 25 Sexual identity by parents'/teachers' expectations of disabled girls having sexual relationships/getting married

Sexual Identity	Don't Know	No	Not Answered	Yes	Grand Total
Bisexual	1.10%	2.21%	0.55%	7.18%	11.05%
Heterosexual	5.52%	29.83%	1.10%	38.67%	75.14%
Lesbian	0.00%	4.42%	0.55%	8.84%	13.81%
Grand Total	**6.63%**	**36.46%**	**2.21%**	**54.70%**	**100.00%**

Fig. 26 Women who attended special school, according to class

Class	No	Not Answered	Partly	Yes	Grand Total
Working	23.20%	0.00%	1.66%	11.60%	36.46%
Middle	38.12%	0.55%	0.00%	15.47%	54.14%
Upper	0.55%	0.00%	0.00%	0.00%	0.55%
Other	2.21%	0.00%	0.00%	0.00%	2.21%
Not Answered	4.42%	0.00%	0.55%	1.66%	6.63%
Grand Total	**68.51%**	**0.55%**	**2.21%**	**28.73%**	**100.00%**

Fig. 27 Women who attended special schools and received sex education

	Little	N/A	No	Not Answered	Yes	Grand Total
No	2.21%	0.55%	27.62%	0.55%	37.57%	68.51%
Not Answered	0.00%	0.00%	0.55%	0.00%	0.00%	0.55%
Partly	0.55%	0.00%	1.66%	0.00%	0.00%	2.21%
Yes	0.55%	0.00%	12.71%	1.10%	14.36%	28.73%
Grand Total	**3.31%**	**0.55%**	**42.54%**	**1.66%**	**51.93%**	**100.00%**

Fig. 27b Ethnic origin by attended special schools and received sex education

Special School	Sex Education	Other	Not Answered	African	Asian	Black British	Caribbean	Irish	White	Grand Total
						Ethnic Origin				
Not Answered	No	0.00%	0.00%	0.00%	0.00%	0.00%	0.00%	0.00%	0.55%	0.55%
Not Answered Total		**0.00%**	**0.00%**	**0.00%**	**0.00%**	**0.00%**	**0.00%**	**0.00%**	**0.55%**	**0.55%**
No	Not Answered	0.00%	0.00%	0.00%	0.00%	0.00%	0.00%	0.00%	0.55%	0.55%
	Little	0.00%	0.55%	0.00%	0.00%	0.00%	0.55%	0.00%	1.10%	2.21%
	N/A	0.00%	0.00%	0.00%	0.00%	0.00%	0.00%	0.00%	0.55%	0.55%
	No	1.66%	2.76%	0.00%	0.00%	0.00%	0.55%	2.76%	19.89%	27.62%
	Yes	1.66%	4.42%	0.55%	1.10%	2.21%	0.55%	0.55%	26.52%	37.57%
No Total		**3.31%**	**7.73%**	**0.55%**	**1.10%**	**2.21%**	**1.66%**	**3.31%**	**48.62%**	**68.51%**
Partly	Little	0.00%	0.00%	0.00%	0.00%	0.00%	0.00%	0.00%	0.55%	0.55%
	No	0.00%	0.55%	0.00%	0.55%	0.00%	0.00%	0.00%	0.55%	1.66%
Partly Total		**0.00%**	**0.55%**	**0.00%**	**0.55%**	**0.00%**	**0.00%**	**0.00%**	**1.10%**	**2.21%**
Yes	Not Answered	0.00%	0.00%	0.00%	0.00%	0.00%	0.00%	0.00%	1.10%	1.10%
	Little	0.00%	0.00%	0.00%	0.00%	0.00%	0.00%	0.00%	0.55%	0.55%
	No	0.55%	1.10%	0.55%	0.55%	0.00%	0.55%	1.66%	7.73%	12.71%
	Yes	0.00%	1.10%	0.00%	0.00%	0.00%	0.55%	0.55%	12.15%	14.36%
Yes Total		**0.55%**	**2.21%**	**0.55%**	**0.55%**	**0.00%**	**1.10%**	**2.21%**	**21.55%**	**28.73%**
Grand Total		**3.87%**	**10.50%**	**1.10%**	**2.21%**	**2.21%**	**2.76%**	**5.52%**	**71.82%**	**100.00%**

Fig. 28 Women wanting more sex information, according to ethnic origin

Ethnic Origin	Don't Know	N/A	No	Not Answered	Yes	Grand Total
African	0.00%	0.00%	0.00%	0.00%	1.10%	1.10%
Asian	0.00%	0.00%	1.66%	0.00%	0.55%	2.21%
Black British	0.00%	0.00%	1.66%	0.55%	0.00%	2.21%
Caribbean	0.00%	0.00%	0.55%	0.00%	2.21%	2.76%
Irish	0.00%	0.00%	2.21%	0.55%	2.76%	5.52%
Not Answered	0.00%	0.00%	3.31%	0.00%	7.18%	10.50%
Other	0.00%	0.00%	2.21%	1.10%	0.55%	3.87%
White	1.10%	0.55%	34.81%	2.76%	32.60%	71.82%
Grand Total	**1.10%**	**0.55%**	**46.41%**	**4.97%**	**46.96%**	**100.00%**

Fig. 29 Women having positive role models, according to ethnic origin

Ethnic Origin	Don't Know	N/A	No	Not Answered	Yes	Grand Total
African	0.00%	0.00%	0.00%	1.10%	0.00%	1.10%
Asian	0.00%	0.00%	1.10%	0.00%	1.10%	2.21%
Black British	0.00%	0.00%	1.10%	1.10%	0.00%	2.21%
Caribbean	0.00%	0.00%	1.66%	0.00%	1.10%	2.76%
Irish	0.00%	0.00%	3.87%	1.10%	0.55%	5.52%
Not Answered	0.00%	0.00%	7.18%	1.10%	2.21%	10.50%
Other	0.00%	0.00%	1.66%	0.00%	2.21%	3.87%
White	1.66%	1.10%	37.57%	2.76%	28.73%	71.82%
Grand Total	**1.66%**	**1.10%**	**54.14%**	**7.18%**	**35.91%**	**100.00%**

Fig. 30 Ethnic origin by practising safer sex

Ethnic Origin	N/A	No	Not Answered	Sometimes	Yes	Grand Total
African	0.00%	0.00%	0.55%	0.00%	0.55%	1.10%
Asian	0.00%	0.55%	0.55%	0.00%	1.10%	2.21%
Black British	0.00%	0.55%	0.55%	0.55%	0.55%	2.21%
Caribbean	0.00%	0.00%	0.00%	0.00%	2.76%	2.76%
Irish	0.00%	3.31%	1.10%	0.00%	1.10%	5.52%
Not Answered	0.00%	6.08%	1.10%	0.00%	3.31%	10.50%
Other	0.00%	0.55%	0.00%	1.10%	2.21%	3.87%
White	9.39%	29.83%	7.73%	1.10%	23.76%	71.82%
Grand Total	**9.39%**	**40.88%**	**11.60%**	**2.76%**	**35.36%**	**100.00%**

Fig. 31 Has religion influenced sexual identity

Sexual Identity	N/A	No	Not Answered	Yes	Grand Total
Heterosexual	1.10%	49.72%	0.55%	23.20%	74.59%
Lesbian	0.00%	10.50%	1.10%	2.21%	13.81%
Bisexual	0.55%	4.42%	0.55%	5.52%	11.05%
Not Answered	0.00%	0.55%	0.00%	0.00%	0.55%
Grand Total	**1.66%**	**65.19%**	**2.21%**	**30.94%**	**100.00%**

Fig. 32 Has sexual identity been influenced by ethnic origin

Ethnic Origin	Don't Know	N/A	No	Not Answered	Yes	Grand Total
African	0.00%	0.00%	0.55%	0.00%	0.55%	1.10%
Asian	0.00%	0.00%	0.00%	0.00%	2.21%	2.21%
Black British	0.00%	0.00%	1.66%	0.00%	0.55%	2.21%
Caribbean	0.00%	0.00%	0.00%	0.00%	2.76%	2.76%
Irish	0.00%	0.00%	3.31%	0.00%	2.21%	5.52%
Not Answered	0.00%	0.00%	8.29%	0.55%	1.66%	10.50%
Other	0.00%	0.00%	1.66%	0.00%	2.21%	3.87%
White	1.10%	0.55%	39.23%	6.08%	24.86%	71.82%
Grand Total	**1.10%**	**0.55%**	**54.70%**	**6.63%**	**37.02%**	**100.00%**

Fig. 33 Family arranging marriage, according to ethnic origin

Ethnic Origin	N/A	No	Not Answered	Yes	Grand Total
African	0.00%	1.10%	0.00%	0.00%	1.10%
Asian	0.00%	1.66%	0.00%	0.55%	2.21%
Black British	0.00%	2.21%	0.00%	0.00%	2.21%
Caribbean	0.00%	2.76%	0.00%	0.00%	2.76%
Irish	0.00%	4.42%	0.00%	1.10%	5.52%
Not Answered	0.00%	9.94%	0.55%	0.00%	10.50%
Other	0.00%	3.31%	0.00%	0.55%	3.87%
White	2.76%	66.30%	1.10%	1.66%	71.82%
Grand Total	**2.76%**	**91.71%**	**1.66%**	**3.87%**	**100.00%**

Fig. 34 Ethnic origin by pressure on sexual choice

Ethnic Origin	N/A	No	Not Answered	Yes	Grand Total
African	0.00%	0.55%	0.00%	0.55%	1.10%
Asian	0.55%	1.66%	0.00%	0.00%	2.21%
Black British	0.55%	1.10%	0.55%	0.00%	2.21%
Caribbean	0.00%	1.66%	0.00%	1.10%	2.76%
Irish	0.55%	2.21%	0.55%	2.21%	5.52%
Not Answered	1.10%	6.08%	2.21%	1.10%	10.50%
Other	0.55%	3.31%	0.00%	0.00%	3.87%
White	4.42%	40.33%	19.34%	7.73%	71.82%
Grand Total	**7.73%**	**56.91%**	**22.65%**	**12.71%**	**100.00%**

Fig. 35 Women who are employed, according to class

Class	N/A	No	Not Answered	Part time	Student	Yes	Grand Total
Working	0.00%	18.23%	0.00%	0.00%	0.55%	17.68%	36.46%
Middle	0.55%	25.41%	0.55%	1.10%	0.00%	26.52%	54.14%
Upper	0.00%	0.55%	0.00%	0.00%	0.00%	0.00%	0.55%
Other	0.00%	2.21%	0.00%	0.00%	0.00%	0.00%	2.21%
Not Answered	0.00%	3.87%	0.00%	0.00%	0.00%	2.76%	6.63%
Grand Total	**0.55%**	**50.28%**	**0.55%**	**1.10%**	**0.55%**	**46.96%**	**100.00%**

Fig. 36 Ethnic origin by women who were born disabled

Ethnic Origin	No	Not Answered	Yes	Grand Total
African	0.55%	0.00%	0.55%	1.10%
Asian	1.66%	0.00%	0.55%	2.21%
Black British	1.66%	0.00%	0.55%	2.21%
Caribbean	2.21%	0.00%	0.55%	2.76%
Irish	2.76%	0.00%	2.76%	5.52%
Not Answered	8.29%	0.00%	2.21%	10.50%
Other	3.31%	0.00%	0.55%	3.87%
White	44.20%	1.10%	26.52%	71.82%
Grand Total	**64.64%**	**1.10%**	**34.25%**	**100.00%**

Fig. 37a) Women who were born disabled, according to sexual identity

Sexual Identity	Not Answered	No	Yes	Grand Total
Hetrosexual	0.55%	45.86%	28.18%	74.59%
Lesbian	0.00%	11.05%	2.76%	13.81%
Bisexual	0.55%	7.18%	3.31%	11.05%
Not Answered	0.00%	0.55%	0.00%	0.55%
Grand Total	**1.10%**	**64.64%**	**34.25%**	**100.00%**

Fig. 37b) Women who were born disabled, according to ethnic origin

Ethnic Origin	Not Answered	No	Yes	Grand Total
African	0.00%	0.55%	0.55%	1.10%
Asian	0.00%	1.66%	0.55%	2.21%
Black British	0.00%	1.66%	0.55%	2.21%
Caribbean	0.00%	2.21%	0.55%	2.76%
Irish	0.00%	2.76%	2.76%	5.52%
Not Answered	0.00%	8.29%	2.21%	10.50%
Other	0.00%	3.31%	0.55%	3.87%
White	1.10%	44.20%	26.52%	71.82%
Grand Total	**1.10%**	**64.64%**	**34.25%**	**100.00%**

Fig. 38 Age when women had first sexual friendship, according to sexual identity

| | Sexual Identity | | | |
Age	Heterosexual	Lesbian	Bisexual	Grand Total
1-5	1	0	0	1
6-10	1	1	0	2
11-15	25	8	8	41
16-20	68	13	8	89
21-25	18	2	1	21
26-30	6	1	1	8
31-35	1	0	0	1
36-40	2	0	2	4
26-30	1	0	0	1
Never	7	0	0	7
Not Answered	6	0	0	6
Grand Total	**136**	**25**	**20**	**181**

Fig 38b Age when women had first sexual friendship, according to ethnic origin

Ethnic Origin	Age											
	Not Answered	1–5	6–10	11–15	16–20	21–25	26–30	31–35	36–40	26–30	Never	Grand Total
Other	0.00%	0.00%	0.00%	1.10%	2.21%	0.55%	0.00%	0.00%	0.00%	0.00%	0.00%	3.87%
Not Answered	0.55%	0.00%	0.00%	1.10%	7.73%	0.00%	0.55%	0.00%	0.00%	0.55%	0.00%	10.50%
African	0.00%	0.00%	0.00%	0.55%	0.00%	0.55%	0.00%	0.00%	0.00%	0.00%	0.00%	1.10%
Asian	0.55%	0.00%	0.00%	0.00%	1.66%	0.00%	0.00%	0.00%	0.00%	0.00%	0.00%	2.21%
Black British	1.10%	0.00%	0.00%	0.00%	0.55%	0.55%	0.00%	0.00%	0.00%	0.00%	0.00%	2.21%
Caribbean	0.00%	0.00%	0.00%	0.55%	1.10%	0.55%	0.55%	0.00%	0.00%	0.00%	0.00%	2.76%
Irish	0.00%	0.00%	0.55%	2.21%	1.10%	1.66%	0.00%	0.00%	0.00%	0.00%	0.00%	5.52%
White	1.10%	0.55%	0.55%	17.13%	34.81%	7.73%	3.31%	0.55%	2.21%	0.00%	3.87%	71.82%
Grand Total	**3.31%**	**0.55%**	**1.10%**	**22.65%**	**49.17%**	**11.60%**	**4.42%**	**0.55%**	**2.21%**	**0.55%**	**3.87%**	**100.00%**

Fig. 39 Age when women first masturbated, according to class

| Age | Class | | | | | |
---	Middle	Not Answered	Other	Upper	Working	Grand Total
1-5	1.10%	0.00%	0.00%	0.00%	2.21%	3.31%
6-10	6.08%	1.66%	0.00%	0.00%	6.08%	13.81%
11-15	12.71%	1.66%	0.00%	0.00%	12.15%	26.52%
16-20	8.84%	1.66%	0.00%	0.00%	6.63%	17.13%
21-25	3.31%	0.00%	0.00%	0.55%	2.21%	6.08%
26-30	1.66%	0.00%	0.00%	0.00%	0.55%	2.21%
31-35	0.55%	0.00%	0.00%	0.00%	0.55%	1.10%
36-40	0.55%	0.00%	0.00%	0.00%	0.00%	0.55%
Don't Know	2.21%	0.55%	1.10%	0.00%	0.55%	4.42%
Never	9.94%	0.55%	0.00%	0.00%	3.31%	13.81%
Not Answered	7.18%	0.55%	1.10%	0.00%	2.21%	11.05%
Grand Total	**54.14%**	**6.63%**	**2.21%**	**0.55%**	**36.46%**	**100.00%**

Fig. 40 Relationships being heterosexual, lesbian or both, according to ethnic origin

Ethnic Origin	Sexual identity					Grand Total
	Heterosexual	Lesbian	Both	N/A	Not Answered	
African	0.00%	0.00%	0.55%	0.00%	0.55%	1.10%
Asian	1.10%	0.00%	0.55%	0.55%	0.00%	2.21%
Black British	0.55%	0.00%	1.10%	0.00%	0.55%	2.21%
Caribbean	1.66%	0.00%	1.10%	0.00%	0.00%	2.76%
Irish	3.31%	0.00%	1.66%	0.00%	0.55%	5.52%
Not Answered	9.39%	0.00%	0.55%	0.00%	0.55%	10.50%
Other	2.76%	0.55%	0.55%	0.00%	0.00%	3.87%
White	45.30%	3.31%	18.23%	2.76%	2.21%	71.82%
Grand Total	**64.09%**	**3.87%**	**24.31%**	**3.31%**	**4.42%**	**100.00%**

Fig. 41 Meeting partners at a club, pub, work or other places, according to class

i) Club

	Class					
	Working	Middle	Upper	Other	Not Answered	Grand Total
N/A	16.57%	34.25%	0.55%	1.66%	2.76%	55.80%
Not Answered	0.00%	0.55%	0.00%	0.00%	0.55%	1.10%
Yes	19.89%	19.34%	0.00%	0.55%	3.31%	43.09%
Grand Total	**36.46%**	**54.14%**	**0.55%**	**2.21%**	**6.63%**	**100.00%**

ii) Pub

	Class					
	Middle	Not Answered	Other	Upper	Working	Grand Total
N/A	34.81%	3.31%	1.66%	0.55%	18.78%	59.12%
Not Answered	0.00%	0.55%	0.00%	0.00%	0.00%	0.55%
Yes	19.34%	2.76%	0.55%	0.00%	17.68%	40.33%
Grand Total	**54.14%**	**6.63%**	**2.21%**	**0.55%**	**36.46%**	**100.00%**

Fig. 41 (cont.)

iii) Work

			Class			
	Middle	Not Answered	Other	Upper	Working	Grand Total
N/A	30.39%	3.31%	1.10%	0.55%	16.57%	51.93%
Not Answered	0.00%	0.55%	0.55%	0.00%	0.00%	1.10%
Yes	23.76%	2.76%	0.55%	0.00%	19.89%	46.96%
Grand Total	**54.14%**	**6.63%**	**2.21%**	**0.55%**	**36.46%**	**100.00%**

iv) Other

			Class			
	Middle	Not Answered	Other	Upper	Working	Grand Total
N/A	12.71%	3.31%	0.00%	0.00%	12.15%	28.18%
Not Answered	0.00%	0.55%	0.00%	0.00%	0.55%	1.10%
Yes	41.44%	2.76%	2.21%	0.55%	23.76%	70.72%
Grand Total	**54.14%**	**6.63%**	**2.21%**	**0.55%**	**36.46%**	**100.00%**

Fig. 41b Meeting partners at a club, pub, work or other places, by ethnic origin

i) Club

	African	Asian	Black British	Caribbean	Irish	Not Answered	Other	White	Grand Total
N/A	0.55%	2.21%	1.10%	1.66%	3.31%	6.63%	2.21%	38.12%	55.80%
Not Answered	0.00%	0.00%	0.55%	0.55%	0.00%	0.00%	0.00%	0.00%	1.10%
Yes	0.55%	0.00%	0.55%	0.55%	2.21%	3.87%	1.66%	33.70%	43.09%
Grand Total	**1.10%**	**2.21%**	**2.21%**	**2.76%**	**5.52%**	**10.50%**	**3.87%**	**71.82%**	**100.00%**

ii) Pub

	African	Asian	Black British	Caribbean	Irish	Not Answered	Other	White	Grand Total
N/A	0.55%	2.21%	1.10%	1.66%	4.97%	7.18%	2.21%	39.23%	59.12%
Not Answered	0.00%	0.00%	0.55%	0.00%	0.00%	0.00%	0.00%	0.00%	0.55%
Yes	0.55%	0.00%	0.55%	1.10%	0.55%	3.31%	1.66%	32.60%	40.33%
Grand Total	**1.10%**	**2.21%**	**2.21%**	**2.76%**	**5.52%**	**10.50%**	**3.87%**	**71.82%**	**100.00%**

Fig. 41b *(cont.)*

iii) Work

	African	Asian	Black British	Caribbean	Irish	Not Answered	Other	White	Grand Total
N/A	0.55%	0.00%	1.10%	1.66%	1.66%	6.63%	1.10%	39.23%	51.93%
Not Answered	0.00%	0.00%	0.55%	0.00%	0.00%	0.00%	0.00%	0.55%	1.10%
Yes	0.55%	2.21%	0.55%	1.10%	3.87%	3.87%	2.76%	32.04%	46.96%
Grand Total	**1.10%**	**2.21%**	**2.21%**	**2.76%**	**5.52%**	**10.50%**	**3.87%**	**71.82%**	**100.00%**

iv) Other

	African	Asian	Black British	Caribbean	Irish	Not Answered	Other	White	Grand Total
N/A	0.00%	1.10%	0.00%	1.66%	2.21%	2.21%	1.66%	19.34%	28.18%
Not Answered	0.00%	0.00%	0.55%	0.00%	0.00%	0.00%	0.00%	0.55%	1.10%
Yes	1.10%	1.10%	1.66%	1.10%	3.31%	8.29%	2.21%	51.93%	70.72%
Grand Total	**1.10%**	**2.21%**	**2.21%**	**2.76%**	**5.52%**	**10.50%**	**3.87%**	**71.82%**	**100.00%**

Fig. 42 Whether partner had a disability, according to ethnic origin

Ethnic Origin	N/A	No	Not Answered	Yes	Grand Total
African	0.00%	1.10%	0.00%	0.00%	1.10%
Asian	1.10%	0.55%	0.00%	0.55%	2.21%
Black British	1.10%	1.10%	0.00%	0.00%	2.21%
Caribbean	1.10%	1.10%	0.00%	0.55%	2.76%
Irish	1.66%	1.66%	0.55%	1.66%	5.52%
Not Answered	1.10%	6.08%	0.00%	3.31%	10.50%
Other	2.76%	1.10%	0.00%	0.00%	3.87%
White	22.65%	32.04%	1.66%	15.47%	71.82%
Grand Total	**31.49%**	**44.75%**	**2.21%**	**21.55%**	**100.00%**

Fig. 43 Reaction from family/friends to able-bodied partner, according to ethnic origin

Ethnic Origin	Both	Don't Know	N/A	Negative	Not Answered	Positive	Grand Total
African	0.55%	0.00%	0.00%	0.00%	0.55%	0.00%	1.10%
Asian	0.00%	0.00%	1.10%	0.00%	0.00%	1.10%	2.21%
Black British	0.00%	0.00%	1.10%	0.00%	0.00%	1.10%	2.21%
Caribbean	0.00%	0.00%	2.21%	0.00%	0.00%	0.55%	2.76%
Irish	0.00%	0.00%	2.76%	0.00%	1.10%	1.66%	5.52%
Not Answered	0.00%	0.00%	3.87%	1.10%	0.55%	4.97%	10.50%
Other	0.00%	0.00%	2.76%	0.00%	0.00%	1.10%	3.87%
White	4.42%	1.66%	29.83%	2.21%	4.42%	29.28%	71.82%
Grand Total	**4.97%**	**1.66%**	**43.65%**	**3.31%**	**6.63%**	**39.78%**	**100.00%**

Fig. 44 Reaction from family/friends to disabled partner, according to ethnic origin

Ethnic Origin	Both	Don't Know	N/A	Negative	Not Answered	Positive	Grand Total
African	0.00%	0.00%	0.55%	0.00%	0.55%	0.00%	1.10%
Asian	0.00%	0.00%	1.66%	0.00%	0.00%	0.55%	2.21%
Black British	0.00%	0.00%	2.21%	0.00%	0.00%	0.00%	2.21%
Caribbean	0.00%	0.00%	2.21%	0.55%	0.00%	0.00%	2.76%
Irish	1.10%	0.00%	3.87%	0.00%	0.55%	0.00%	5.52%
Not Answered	0.00%	0.00%	6.08%	0.55%	1.10%	2.76%	10.50%
Other	0.00%	0.00%	3.31%	0.55%	0.00%	0.00%	3.87%
White	2.76%	0.55%	46.96%	3.31%	5.52%	12.71%	71.82%
Grand Total	**3.87%**	**0.55%**	**66.85%**	**4.97%**	**7.73%**	**16.02%**	**100.00%**

Fig. 45 Numbers of sexual partners, according to sexual identity

Nos of Partners

Sexual Identity	0	1	2	3	4	5	6	7	8	9	10	11	12	13	15	18	20	24	25	27	30	50	100	DK	Many	N/A	Not Ans	Grand Total
Heterosexual	11	30	15	8	6	11	12	6	6	2	7	1	1	1	1	0	5	0	1	0	0	1	0	0	1	4	6	136
Lesbian	0	0	4	0	4	1	3	1	0	0	1	0	0	0	0	1	2	1	0	1	1	1	0	1	1	2	0	25
Bisexual	0	1	2	1	1	2	0	3	1	0	3	0	0	0	0	0	0	0	1	0	0	0	1	0	0	1	2	20
Grand Total	**11**	**31**	**21**	**9**	**11**	**14**	**15**	**10**	**7**	**2**	**11**	**1**	**1**	**1**	**1**	**1**	**7**	**1**	**2**	**1**	**1**	**2**	**1**	**1**	**2**	**7**	**8**	**181**

Fig. 46 Sex difficulties due to physical reasons, according to sexual identity

Sexual Identity	Don't Know	N/A	No	Not Answered	Yes	Grand Total
Heterosexual	0.55%	1.10%	38.67%	4.42%	30.39%	75.14%
Lesbian	0.00%	0.55%	3.31%	0.55%	9.39%	13.81%
Bisexual	0.00%	0.00%	4.97%	0.55%	5.52%	11.05%
Grand Total	**0.55%**	**1.66%**	**46.96%**	**5.52%**	**45.30%**	**100.00%**

Fig. 47 Rejection on being disabled, according to sexual identity

Sexual Identity	Don't Know	N/A	No	Not Answered	Yes	Grand Total
Heterosexual	1.10%	13.81%	37.57%	15.47%	7.18%	75.14%
Lesbian	0.00%	2.76%	6.08%	2.21%	2.76%	13.81%
Bisexual	0.00%	1.10%	6.63%	2.21%	1.10%	11.05%
Grand Total	**1.10%**	**17.68%**	**50.28%**	**19.89%**	**11.05%**	**100.00%**

Fig. 48 Understanding information about sex, according to class

Class	N/A	No	Not Answered	Sometimes	Yes	Grand Total
Working	0.00%	2.21%	0.00%	0.00%	34.25%	36.46%
Middle	0.55%	4.42%	1.66%	0.55%	46.96%	54.14%
Upper	0.00%	0.00%	0.00%	0.00%	0.55%	0.55%
Other	0.00%	0.55%	0.55%	0.00%	1.10%	2.21%
Not Answered	0.00%	0.55%	0.00%	0.00%	6.08%	6.63%
Grand Total	**0.55%**	**7.73%**	**2.21%**	**0.55%**	**88.95%**	**100.00%**

Fig. 49 Women wanting to discuss sex in a safe environment, according to sexual identity

Sexual Identity	Don't Know	N/A	No	Not Answered	Yes	Grand Total
Heterosexual	2.21%	0.55%	25.41%	4.42%	42.54%	75.14%
Lesbian	0.00%	0.00%	2.21%	0.55%	11.05%	13.81%
Bisexual	0.55%	0.00%	3.87%	2.21%	4.42%	11.05%
Grand Total	**2.76%**	**0.55%**	**31.49%**	**7.18%**	**58.01%**	**100.00%**

Fig. 49b Women wanting to discuss sex in a safe environment, according to ethnic origin

Ethnic Origin	Not Answered	Don't Know	N/A	No	Yes	Grand Total
African	0.55%	0.00%	0.00%	0.00%	0.55%	1.10%
Asian	0.00%	0.55%	0.00%	0.00%	1.66%	2.21%
Black British	1.10%	0.00%	0.00%	1.10%	0.00%	2.21%
Caribbean	0.00%	0.55%	0.00%	0.00%	2.21%	2.76%
Irish	0.55%	0.00%	0.00%	1.66%	3.31%	5.52%
Not Answered	0.00%	0.00%	0.00%	3.87%	6.63%	10.50%
Other	0.55%	0.00%	0.00%	1.10%	2.21%	3.87%
White	4.42%	1.66%	0.55%	23.76%	41.44%	71.82%
Grand Total	**7.18%**	**2.76%**	**0.55%**	**31.49%**	**58.01%**	**100.00%**

Fig. 50 Women wanting to talk about sex, in a group, according to sex identity

Sexual Identity	Don't Know	Maybe	No	Not Answered	Yes	Grand Total
Heterosexual	1.66%	1.10%	20.44%	2.76%	48.62%	74.59%
Lesbian	0.00%	0.55%	2.21%	0.00%	11.05%	13.81%
Bisexual	0.00%	0.00%	1.66%	0.55%	8.84%	11.05%
Not Answered	0.00%	0.00%	0.00%	0.00%	0.55%	0.55%
Grand Total	**1.66%**	**1.66%**	**24.31%**	**3.31%**	**69.06%**	**100.00%**

Fig. 50b Women wanting to talk about sex, in a group, according to ethnic origin

Ethnic Origin	Not Answered	Don't Know	Maybe	No	Yes	Grand Total
African	1	0	0	0	1	2
Asian	0	1	0	0	3	4
Black British	0	0	0	2	2	4
Caribbean	0	0	0	0	5	5
Irish	2	0	0	2	6	10
Not Answered	0	0	0	9	10	19
Other	0	0	0	2	5	7
White	3	2	3	29	93	130
Grand Total	**6**	**3**	**3**	**44**	**125**	**181**

Fig. 51 Need to discuss sex on a one to one basis, according to sexual identity

Sexual Identity	Don't Know	Maybe	No	Not Answered	Yes	Grand Total
Heterosexual	0.55%	1.66%	53.04%	3.31%	16.57%	75.14%
Lesbian	0.00%	0.00%	10.50%	1.66%	1.66%	13.81%
Bisexual	0.00%	0.00%	6.63%	2.76%	1.66%	11.05%
Grand Total	**0.55%**	**1.66%**	**70.17%**	**7.73%**	**19.89%**	**100.00%**

Fig. 51b Need to discuss sex on a one-to-one basis, according to ethnic origin

Ethnic Origin	Not Answered	Don't Know	Maybe	No	Yes	Grand Total
African	0.55%	0.00%	0.00%	0.00%	0.55%	1.10%
Asian	0.00%	0.00%	0.55%	1.66%	0.00%	2.21%
Black British	0.55%	0.00%	0.00%	1.66%	0.00%	2.21%
Caribbean	0.00%	0.00%	0.00%	0.55%	2.21%	2.76%
Irish	1.10%	0.00%	0.00%	3.31%	1.10%	5.52%
Not Answered	0.55%	0.00%	0.00%	7.73%	2.21%	10.50%
Other	0.00%	0.00%	0.00%	3.31%	0.55%	3.87%
White	4.97%	0.55%	1.10%	51.93%	13.26%	71.82%
Grand Total	**7.73%**	**0.55%**	**1.66%**	**70.17%**	**19.89%**	**100.00%**

Fig. 52 Discouraged from having sex due to impairment, according to sexual identity

Sexual Identity	No	Not Answered	Yes	Grand Total
Heterosexual	56.35%	1.66%	17.13%	75.14%
Lesbian	10.50%	1.10%	2.21%	13.81%
Bisexual	8.29%	1.10%	1.66%	11.05%
Grand Total	**75.14%**	**3.87%**	**20.99%**	**100.00%**

Fig. 52b Discouraged from having sex due to impairment, according to ethnic origin

Ethnic Origin	Not Answered	No	Yes	Grand Total
African	0.55%	0.55%	0.00%	1.10%
Asian	0.00%	2.21%	0.00%	2.21%
Black British	0.00%	2.21%	0.00%	2.21%
Caribbean	0.00%	1.66%	1.10%	2.76%
Irish	0.55%	4.42%	0.55%	5.52%
Not Answered	0.00%	8.29%	2.21%	10.50%
Other	0.00%	3.31%	0.55%	3.87%
White	2.76%	52.49%	16.57%	71.82%
Grand Total	**3.87%**	**75.14%**	**20.99%**	**100.00%**

Fig. 53 Ridiculed because of impairment, according to sexual identity

Sexual Identity	No	Not Answered	Yes	Grand Total
Bisexual	8.29%	1.66%	1.10%	11.05%
Heterosexual	48.62%	2.76%	23.76%	75.14%
Lesbian	9.39%	1.10%	3.31%	13.81%
Grand Total	**66.30%**	**5.52%**	**28.18%**	**100.00%**

Fig. 53b Ridiculed because of impairment, according to ethnic origin

Ethnic Origin	Not Answered	No	Yes	Grand Total
African	0.55%	0.55%	0.00%	1.10%
Asian	0.00%	0.55%	1.66%	2.21%
Black British	0.55%	0.55%	1.10%	2.21%
Caribbean	0.00%	1.10%	1.66%	2.76%
Irish	1.10%	2.76%	1.66%	5.52%
Not Answered	0.00%	8.84%	1.66%	10.50%
Other	0.00%	2.76%	1.10%	3.87%
White	3.31%	49.17%	19.34%	71.82%
Grand Total	**5.52%**	**66.30%**	**28.18%**	**100.00%**

Fig 54

i) Sexual identity and having sexual fantasies

Sexual Identity	Don't Know	No	Not Answered	Sometimes	Yes	Grand Total
Heterosexual	0.55%	13.26%	2.21%	1.10%	58.01%	75.14%
Lesbian	0.00%	0.55%	0.55%	0.00%	12.71%	13.81%
Bisexual	0.00%	1.10%	0.55%	0.00%	9.39%	11.05%
Grand Total	**0.55%**	**14.92%**	**3.31%**	**1.10%**	**80.11%**	**100.00%**

ii) Sexual identity and having impairments in fantasies

Sexual Identity	Don't Know	N/A	No	Not Answered	Sometimes	Yes	Grand Total
Heterosexual	0.55%	7.73%	43.09%	8.84%	3.87%	11.05%	75.14%
Lesbian	0.00%	1.10%	6.63%	1.66%	1.66%	2.76%	13.81%
Bisexual	0.00%	1.10%	4.97%	1.66%	2.76%	0.55%	11.05%
Grand Total	**0.55%**	**9.94%**	**54.70%**	**12.15%**	**8.29%**	**14.36%**	**100.00%**

iii) Sexual identity and enjoying fantasies more than sex

Sexual Identity	Don't Know	N/A	No	Not Answered	Sometimes	Yes	Grand Total
Heterosexual	1.10%	7.18%	43.09%	8.29%	3.31%	12.15%	75.14%
Lesbian	0.00%	0.55%	10.50%	0.00%	2.21%	0.55%	13.81%
Bisexual	0.00%	0.00%	7.18%	1.10%	2.21%	0.55%	11.05%
Grand Total	**1.10%**	**7.73%**	**60.77%**	**9.39%**	**7.73%**	**13.26%**	**100.00%**

Fig. 55

i) Using sex toys, according to sexual identity

Sexual Identity	N/A	No	Not Answered	Yes	Grand Total
Heterosexual	1.10%	55.80%	3.87%	14.36%	75.14%
Lesbian	0.00%	5.52%	0.00%	8.29%	13.81%
Bisexual	0.00%	4.97%	0.55%	5.52%	11.05%
Grand Total	**1.10%**	**66.30%**	**4.42%**	**28.18%**	**100.00%**

ii) The use of sex toys to help with impairment, according to sexual identity

Sexual Identity	N/A	No	Not Answered	Yes	Grand Total
Heterosexual	44.20%	23.20%	4.97%	2.76%	75.14%
Lesbian	3.31%	8.29%	0.55%	1.66%	13.81%
Bisexual	2.76%	6.63%	1.10%	0.55%	11.05%
Grand Total	**50.28%**	**38.12%**	**6.63%**	**4.97%**	**100.00%**

Fig. 56

i) Needing help when having sex, according to sexual identity

Sexual Identity	Don't Know	N/A	No	Not Answered	Sometimes	Yes	Grand Total
Bisexual	0.00%	0.00%	8.84%	0.55%	0.55%	1.10%	11.05%
Heterosexual	0.55%	7.18%	54.70%	10.50%	0.55%	1.66%	75.14%
Lesbian	0.00%	0.55%	11.05%	0.55%	0.55%	1.10%	13.81%
Grand Total	**0.55%**	**7.73%**	**74.59%**	**11.60%**	**1.66%**	**3.87%**	**100.00%**

ii) Who assists when having sex, according to sexual identity

Sexual Identity	Friends	N/A	No	Not Answered	Partner	Grand Total
Bisexual	0.00%	7.73%	1.10%	1.66%	0.55%	11.05%
Heterosexual	0.00%	59.67%	3.87%	8.84%	2.76%	75.14%
Lesbian	0.55%	9.94%	1.10%	0.55%	1.66%	13.81%
Grand Total	**0.55%**	**77.35%**	**6.08%**	**11.05%**	**4.97%**	**100.00%**

Fig. 57

i) Expected to get pregnant, according to class

Class	Don't Know	N/A	No	Not Answered	Yes	Grand Total
Working	1.10%	0.00%	16.57%	2.76%	16.02%	36.46%
Middle	0.55%	2.21%	23.20%	4.42%	23.76%	54.14%
Upper	0.00%	0.00%	0.55%	0.00%	0.00%	0.55%
Other	0.00%	0.00%	0.55%	0.00%	1.66%	2.21%
Not Answered	0.00%	0.00%	3.87%	1.10%	1.66%	6.63%
Grand Total	**1.66%**	**2.21%**	**44.75%**	**8.29%**	**43.09%**	**100.00%**

ii) Women having had an abortion, according to class

Class	N/A	No	Not Answered	Yes	Grand Total
Working	0.00%	32.60%	0.00%	3.87%	36.46%
Middle	0.55%	47.51%	1.10%	4.97%	54.14%
Upper	0.00%	0.55%	0.00%	0.00%	0.55%
Other	0.00%	1.10%	0.55%	0.55%	2.21%
Not Answered	0.00%	5.52%	0.55%	0.55%	6.63%
Grand Total	**0.55%**	**87.29%**	**2.21%**	**9.94%**	**100.00%**

iii) Pressure to abort from medical profession, according to class

Class	N/A	No	Not Answered	Yes	Grand Total
Working	12.71%	16.02%	3.31%	4.42%	36.46%
Middle	17.13%	30.39%	2.76%	3.87%	54.14%
Upper	0.00%	0.55%	0.00%	0.00%	0.55%
Other	0.55%	0.55%	1.10%	0.00%	2.21%
Not Answered	2.21%	1.66%	1.10%	1.66%	6.63%
Grand Total	**32.60%**	**49.17%**	**8.29%**	**9.94%**	**100.00%**

iv) Medical support of pregnancy, according to class

Class	N/A	No	Not Answered	Yes	Grand Total
Working	14.92%	3.87%	6.08%	11.60%	36.46%
Middle	26.52%	3.87%	8.84%	14.92%	54.14%
Upper	0.00%	0.00%	0.55%	0.00%	0.55%
Other	0.00%	0.00%	0.55%	1.66%	2.21%
Not Answered	1.66%	1.10%	1.10%	2.76%	6.63%
Grand Total	**43.09%**	**8.84%**	**17.13%**	**30.94%**	**100.00%**

Fig. 58

i) Women wanting to adopt, according to class

Class	Don't Know	N/A	No	Not Answered	Yes	Grand Total
Working	0.00%	1.10%	18.23%	2.21%	14.92%	36.46%
Middle	0.55%	1.66%	33.70%	5.52%	12.71%	54.14%
Upper	0.00%	0.00%	0.55%	0.00%	0.00%	0.55%
Other	0.00%	0.00%	1.10%	0.00%	1.10%	2.21%
Not Answered	0.00%	0.00%	3.31%	1.66%	1.66%	6.63%
Grand Total	**0.55%**	**2.76%**	**56.91%**	**9.39%**	**30.39%**	**100.00%**

ii) Reaction women received to adoption, according to class

Class	Mixed	N/A	Negative	Not Answered	Not tried yet	Positive	Grand Total
Working	0.55%	21.55%	4.42%	5.52%	3.31%	1.10%	36.46%
Middle	0.00%	36.46%	6.63%	6.63%	2.76%	1.66%	54.14%
Upper	0.00%	0.55%	0.00%	0.00%	0.00%	0.00%	0.55%
Other	0.55%	1.10%	0.00%	0.00%	0.00%	0.55%	2.21%
Not Answered	0.00%	3.87%	0.55%	1.66%	0.00%	0.55%	6.63%
Grand Total	**1.10%**	**63.54%**	**11.60%**	**13.81%**	**6.08%**	**3.87%**	**100.00%**

Fig. 59

i) Told not to try for children, according to class

Class	N/A	No	Not Answered	Yes	Grand Total
Working	1.10%	21.55%	2.21%	11.60%	36.46%
Middle	2.76%	32.60%	6.08%	12.71%	54.14%
Upper	0.00%	0.55%	0.00%	0.00%	0.55%
Other	0.00%	1.66%	0.00%	0.55%	2.21%
Not Answered	0.00%	2.76%	1.66%	2.21%	6.63%
Grand Total	**3.87%**	**59.12%**	**9.94%**	**27.07%**	**100.00%**

ii) Medical reasons for being told not to try for children, according to class

Class	Don't Know	N/A	No	Not Answered	Yes	Grand Total
Working	1.10%	13.26%	12.15%	3.31%	6.63%	36.46%
Middle	1.10%	19.89%	14.36%	9.94%	8.84%	54.14%
Upper	0.00%	0.00%	0.00%	0.55%	0.00%	0.55%
Other	0.00%	1.10%	0.55%	0.00%	0.55%	2.21%
Not Answered	0.55%	0.55%	2.21%	1.66%	1.66%	6.63%
Grand Total	**2.76%**	**34.81%**	**29.28%**	**15.47%**	**17.68%**	**100.00%**

Fig. 60

i) Wanting to abort a disabled baby, according to class

Class	Don't Know	Maybe	N/A	No	Not Answered	Yes	Grand Total
Working	1.66%	2.76%	0.55%	25.41%	1.10%	4.97%	36.46%
Middle	3.31%	5.52%	1.66%	30.39%	4.42%	8.84%	54.14%
Upper	0.00%	0.00%	0.00%	0.00%	0.00%	0.55%	0.55%
Other	0.00%	0.55%	0.00%	1.10%	0.55%	0.00%	2.21%
Not Answered	0.00%	1.10%	0.00%	3.31%	1.66%	0.55%	6.63%
Grand Total	**4.97%**	**9.94%**	**2.21%**	**60.22%**	**7.73%**	**14.92%**	**100.00%**

ii) Consider being a single parent, according to class

Class	N/A	No	Not Answered	Yes	Grand Total
Working	0.55%	13.81%	0.55%	21.55%	36.46%
Middle	1.10%	24.86%	3.87%	24.31%	54.14%
Upper	0.00%	0.55%	0.00%	0.00%	0.55%
Other	0.00%	0.55%	0.00%	1.66%	2.21%
Not Answered	0.00%	3.31%	1.10%	2.21%	6.63%
Grand Total	**1.66%**	**43.09%**	**5.52%**	**49.72%**	**100.00%**

Fig. 61 Comfortable with ability to express sexuality, according to ethnic origin

Ethnic Origin	Don't Know	No	Not Answered	Sometimes	Yes	Grand Total
African	0.00%	0.00%	0.00%	0.00%	1.10%	1.10%
Asian	0.00%	0.55%	0.00%	0.00%	1.66%	2.21%
Black British	0.00%	0.55%	0.00%	0.00%	1.66%	2.21%
Caribbean	0.00%	1.10%	0.00%	0.00%	1.66%	2.76%
Irish	0.00%	1.10%	0.55%	0.55%	3.31%	5.52%
Not Answered	0.00%	2.76%	1.10%	0.00%	6.63%	10.50%
Other	0.00%	0.00%	0.00%	0.00%	3.87%	3.87%
White	0.55%	17.13%	5.52%	4.97%	43.65%	71.82%
Grand Total	**0.55%**	**23.20%**	**7.18%**	**5.52%**	**63.54%**	**100.00%**

Fig. 62 Class by how do you rate your confidence

i) At Work

Confidence at work	Working	Middle	Upper	Other	Not Answered	Grand Total
High	10.50%	17.68%	0.00%	0.55%	1.10%	29.83%
Low	0.55%	6.08%	0.00%	0.00%	1.10%	7.73%
Mod	17.68%	17.68%	0.55%	0.55%	3.87%	40.33%
N/A	7.73%	11.60%	0.00%	1.10%	0.55%	20.99%
Not Answered	0.00%	1.10%	0.00%	0.00%	0.00%	1.10%
Grand Total	**36.46%**	**54.14%**	**0.55%**	**2.21%**	**6.63%**	**100.00%**

ii) At Home

Confidence at home	Working	Middle	Upper	Other	Not Answered	Grand Total
High	20.99%	32.04%	0.00%	1.10%	4.97%	59.12%
Low	4.42%	3.31%	0.00%	0.00%	0.00%	7.73%
Mod	11.05%	17.68%	0.55%	1.10%	1.66%	32.04%
Not Answered	0.00%	1.10%	0.00%	0.00%	0.00%	1.10%
Grand Total	**36.46%**	**54.14%**	**0.55%**	**2.21%**	**6.63%**	**100.00%**

iii) With Lover

Confidence with lover	Working	Middle	Upper	Other	Not Answered	Grand Total
High	13.81%	24.31%	0.00%	0.55%	1.66%	40.33%
Low	4.42%	3.31%	0.55%	0.00%	1.10%	9.39%
Mod	13.26%	12.15%	0.00%	1.10%	2.76%	29.28%
N/A	4.97%	13.26%	0.00%	0.55%	1.10%	19.89%
Not Answered	0.00%	1.10%	0.00%	0.00%	0.00%	1.10%
Grand Total	**36.46%**	**54.14%**	**0.55%**	**2.21%**	**6.63%**	**100.00%**

iv) Socialising

Confidence socialising	Working	Middle	Upper	Other	Not Answered	Grand Total
High	13.26%	16.57%	0.00%	0.00%	1.10%	30.94%
Low	8.29%	11.60%	0.55%	0.55%	0.55%	21.55%
Mod	14.92%	24.31%	0.00%	1.66%	4.97%	45.86%
N/A	0.00%	0.55%	0.00%	0.00%	0.00%	0.55%
Not Answered	0.00%	1.10%	0.00%	0.00%	0.00%	1.10%
Grand Total	**36.46%**	**54.14%**	**0.55%**	**2.21%**	**6.63%**	**100.00%**

Useful contacts

The organisations listed below deal with at least some of the issues raised within the report. As most are self-financing and under-resourced, please enclose a stamped addressed envelope when making an enquiry in writing (one International Reply Coupon if writing from outside the United Kingdom).

Disability organisations

British Council of Organisations of Disabled People (BCODP)
Litchurch Plaza
Litchurch Lane
Derby DE24 8AA
Tel. 01332 295551

BCODP is an umbrella organisation for all organisations controlled by disabled people. Contact them direct for a list of their member groups.

British Deaf Association
1-3 Worship Street
London EC2A 2AB
Tel. (0171) 588 3520 (voice), (0171) 588 3529 (Minicom)
FAX (0171) 588 3327

Membership-led organisation with regional groups (see below for main contacts). Newsletter and magazine (*British Deaf News*). Annual members' conference.

British Deaf Association Wales
Shand House
2 Fitzalan Place
Cardiff CF2 1BD
Tel. (01222) 499 873 (voice), (01222) 488 437 (Minicom)
FAX (01222) 499 873

British Deaf Association Scotland
Glasgow Centre for the Deaf
100 Norfolk Street
Glasgow G5 9EJ
Tel. (0141) 420 1878 (Minicom)
FAX (0141) 420 1960

DIAL, UK
Park Lodge
St Catherine's Hospital
Tickhill Road
Doncaster DN4 8QN
Tel. and Minicom (01302) 310123
FAX (01302) 310404

Disablement information & advice lines. National headquarters of federation of telephone helplines. This office can supply help with running disability advice centres and provide staff training and welfare rights advice support. Monthly newsletter for affiliated groups. For services specifically for deaf people, see British Deaf Association, which (at time of going to press) is setting up 'Deaf DIAL' based within its own branches.

SPOD
286 Camden Road
Holloway
London N7 0BJ
Tel. (0171) 607 8851

Sexual and personal relationships of people with a disability. Help and advice. Various publications, including newsletter.

Lesbian & gay organisations

For details of local groups contact your local Lesbian & Gay Switchboard or branch of Friend (Cara/Friend in Ireland). Some national groups have local branches.

Bisexual Helpline
Tel. (0181) 569 7500, Tue and Wed, 7.30–9.30pm

Black Lesbian & Gay Centre Project
BM Box 4390
London WC1N 3XX
Tel. (0181) 885 3543, Thur, 6–9pm
Brothers & Sisters
c/o 77 Lullington Road
Anerley
London SE20 8DG

Lesbian and gay group for deaf and hard-of-hearing people.

Friend
BM National Friend
London WC1N 3XX

National counselling service for lesbians and gay men. Details of local branches can be obtained from this address.

Gay Visually Impaired Group
23 Ballard Court
Bury Road
Gosport
Hants. PO12 3UA
Tel. (01705) 524739

Gemma
BM Box 5700,
London WC1N 3XX

National friendship group for lesbian and bisexual women with/without disabilities. Penfriend service and quarterly newsletter. Enquiries on tape or in Braille welcome.

Irish Gay Helpline
BM IGHm
London WC1N 3XX
Tel. (0181) 983 4111, Mon (evenings).

Lesbian & Gay Youth Movement
BM GYM
London WC1N 3XX
Tel. (0181) 317 9690

National network of groups and youth clubs for lesbian, gay and bisexual people under 26.

Lesbian Information Service
PO Box 8
Todmorden
Lancs. OL14 5TZ
Tel. (01706) 817235

London Lesbian Line
BM Box 1514
London WC1N 3XX
Tel. (0171) 251 6900 Mon and Fri, 2–10pm, Tue–Thu, 7–10pm

Can give details of your nearest lesbian lines, social groups, etc. anywhere in the UK.

National Lesbian & Gay Switchboard
PO Box 7324
London N1
Tel. (0171) 837 7324

24-hour information and advice service. Can supply details of local groups.

PACE
34 Hartman Road
Holloway
London N7 9JL
Tel. (0171) 700 1323

Project for advice, counselling and education.
REGARD
BM Regard
London WC1N 3XX

National campaigning group for disabled lesbians and gay men.

SHAKTI
BM Box 3167
London WC1N 3XX
Tel. (0181) 802 8981 or (0181) 885 3543

Asian lesbian and gay network.

Stonewall
16 Clerkenwell Close
London EC1R 0AA
Tel. (0171) 336 8860
FAX (0171) 336 8864
E-mail: infor@stonewall.org.uk

National campaigning group. Various activities, including Parenting Group.

Parents' organisations

My Mum's Group
Babs Greenwood,
Flat 5
1 South View
Teignmouth
Devon TQ14 8BJ

Support group for lesbian mothers.

Stonewall Parenting Group – see Stonewall, above.

Religious organisations

The following are liberal religious groups with an interest in lesbian and gay and/or disability issues.

Christian Young Gay Network
158 Sterling Gardens
New Cross
London SE14 6DZ

For under-30s.

Friends, Religious Society of
Friends House
Euston Road
London NW1 2BT
Tel. (0171) 387 3601

National Quaker headquarters. Can supply information on local congregations and special interest groups.

Jewish Lesbian & Gay Group
BM JGLG
London WC1N 3XX
Tel. (0181) 848 7319, Mon–Fri, 9am–9pm;
24-hour talking newsletter: (0171) 224 9037.

Non-denominational social group.

Jewish Lesbian & Gay Helpline
BM Jewish Helpline
London WC1N 3XX
Tel. (0171) 706 3123, Mon and Thu, 7–10pm, except Festivals and Holidays.

National information and support service.

Lesbian & Gay Christian Movement
Oxford House
Derbyshire Street
London E2 6HG
Tel. & FAX (0171) 739 1249

Non-denominational. Has many local groups and supplies wide range of publications available by mail order.

Metropolitan Community Church

Non-denominational Christian church with special ministry to the lesbian and gay community.

Quest
BM Box 2585
London WC1N 3XX
Helpline (0171) 792 0274 Fri to Sun, 7–10pm

Lesbian and gay Catholic group.

Unitarian Headquarters
(Information Department)
Essex Hall
1–6 Essex Street,
London WC2R 3HY
Tel. (0171) 240 2384
FAX (0171) 240 3089
E-mail: ga@unitarian.org.uk

Can arrange child-naming ceremonies and blessings of same-sex relationships. Maintains contact with liberal religious groups from non-Christian traditions (e.g. Hindu, Jewish, Buddhist).

Sex education

AIDS Ahead
British Deaf Association
1–3 Worship Street
London EC2A 2AB
Tel. (0171) 588 3521 (voice), (0171) 588 3580 (Minicom)
FAX (0171) 588 3523

Help and advice on AIDS, HIV and related issues for deaf and hard-of-hearing people. Full service for people whose first language is BSL. Employs volunteers throughout the UK, 75 per cent of whom are deaf. Training for qualifications in counselling is encouraged.

British Deaf Association
Health Promotion Service
17 Macon Court
Herald Drive`
Crewe
Cheshire CW1 6EE
Tel. (01270) 250736 (voice), (01270) 250743 (Minicom)
FAX (01270) 250742

A range of services to deaf and hard-of-hearing people, including counselling. The Minicom Helpline (specifically for counselling) is open Wed 7–10pm. Answering machines operate outside the times of this session and office hours. Full service for people whose first language is BSL. See 'AIDS Ahead'.

Brook Advisory Centres
165 Gray's Inn Road
London WC1X 8UD
Tel. (0171) 713 9000
24-Hour Automated Helpline (0171) 617 8000

National help and information service for young people on sexual health and birth control. Many local branches.

Deaf Action on Sexual Health (DASH) – See AIDS Ahead (same details).
Sex Education Forum
National Children's Bureau
8 Wakley Street
London EC1V 7QE
Tel. (0171) 843 6052

National coalition of voluntary organisations concerned with sexual health, contraception, etc. including lesbian and gay groups and health care professionals' associations. Has book sales department which covers specialist subjects, including particular disabilities. Tel. (0171) 843 6028/29; e-mail: booksales@ncb.org.uk